Joseph Edward Adams Smith

The Poet Among the Hills

Oliver Wendell Holmes in Berkshire

Joseph Edward Adams Smith

The Poet Among the Hills
Oliver Wendell Holmes in Berkshire

ISBN/EAN: 9783337006365

Printed in Europe, USA, Canada, Australia, Japan

Cover: Foto ©Thomas Meinert / pixelio.de

More available books at **www.hansebooks.com**

THE POET AMONG THE HILLS.

OLIVER WENDELL HOLMES
IN BERKSHIRE.

His Berkshire Poems, some of them now first published, with Historic and Descriptive Incidents Concerning the Poems, the Poet, and his Literary Neighbors. His Poetic, Personal and Ancestral Relations to the County.

BY

J. E. A. SMITH.

"The memory of great men is the noblest inheritance of their country."

PITTSFIELD, MASS.:
GEORGE BLATCHFORD.
1895.

"Whatever strengthens our local attachments is favorable both to individual and to national character. Our home, our birthplace, our native land,—think for a while what the virtues are which arise out of the feelings connected with these words. . . . Show me a man who cares no more for one place than another, and I will show you in that same person one who loves nothing but himself. Beware of those who are homeless by choice: you have no hold on a human being whose affections are without a tap-root."—SOUTHEY: *The Doctor.*

TABLE OF CONTENTS.

PAGE

PROLOGUE.—Why and Because—Dr. Holmes' Berkshire Poetry Characterized—Fable of a Socialist Community—What Pittsfield is Proud of—Berkshire Scenery—A Haunt for Literary Lions—Melville and Hawthorne—Longfellow, the Old Clock on the Stairs, Roaring Brook and Kavanagh, Charles Sumner and Fanny Kemble—Dr. Holmes and the Newspaper Press, . . 7

I. BERKSHIRE JUBILEE SPEECH AND POEM.—Sketch of the Jubilee—The Dinner—David Dudley Field's Journey of a Day—Catherine Sedgwick's Chronicles—Dr. Holmes' Speech from a Table—His Poem of Welcome, . . . 49

II. THE WENDELL FAMILY.—Jacob Wendell's Descent—Jacob Wendell in Boston—Connection with Old Boston Families—His Descendants—Holmes Genealogy — Phillips Genealogy—Wendell Phillips—Oliver Wendell in Pittsfield—Curious Incidents—Oliver Wendell Fierce for Moderation; Friendship for Henry and Peter Van Schaack, ... 69

III. DR. HOLMES' SUMMER VILLA, AND LIFE IN IT.—The Villa—Letters to a Pittsfield Lady and Her Reminiscences—Letter to a School-Teacher—Blackberries and Other Berries—The Canoe Meadows—The Holmes Pine, . . . 87

IV. A VISION OF THE HOUSATONIC RIVER.—Dr. Holmes' Love for the River—Remembered by the Classic Cam in England—River Loved by Many Men and Women of Letters—The Vision, 98

TABLE OF CONTENTS.

PAGE

V. YOUNG LADIES' INSTITUTE POEM.—Character of the Institute—John Quincy Adams Visits It—Graduating Exercises in 1849—Speech by Ex-President John Tyler—Dr. Holmes' Speech and Poem, ... 106

VI. THE PLOUGHMAN.—Genesis of the Berkshire Agricultural Society—Elkanah Watson—Major Thomas Melville—John Quincy Adams on Agricultural Oratory—The Picturesque First Cattle Show—How Women Used to Receive Their Premiums—About Ploughing Matches—Cattle Shows of 1849 and 1851—Dr. Holmes' Report on Ploughing Match—His Poem, "The Ploughman," 114

VII. THE PITTSFIELD CEMETERY DEDICATION POEM.—Description of Cemetery Grounds—Previous Burial Grounds—Dedication Exercises—Quotation from Rev. Dr. Neill's Address—Dr. Holmes and Wendell Phillips—Dedication Poem, ... 135

VIII. THE NEW EDEN.—How the Poem Was Written, ... 145

IX. POEMS FOR LADIES' FAIR.—St. Stephen's Church Fair—A Lady's Raid on Dr. Holmes' Poetical Preserves—Camilla—Portia's Leaden Casket—What a Dollar Will Buy, ... 151

X. L'ENVOI.—The Mountains and the Sea—Presentation from Dr. Holmes' Library to Berkshire Athenæum — Hawthorne's Desk — Pittsfield Characters in Dr. Holmes' Novels—Good-By, Old Folks! 159

XI. APPENDIX.—Longfellow's Poem, "The Old Clock on the Stairs;" Fanny Kemble's Ode for the Berkshire Jubilee. "A Berkshire Summer Morning—A Quaint Old Cattle-Show Program, 169

THE POET AMONG THE HILLS.

PROLOGUE.

Why and Because—Dr. Holmes' Berkshire Poetry Characterized—What Pittsfield is Proud of—Fable of a Socialist Community—Berkshire Scenery—A Haunt for Literary Lions—Melville and Hawthorne—Longfellow, the Old Clock on the Stairs, and Roaring Brook—Charles Sumner and Fanny Kemble—Dr. Holmes and the Newspaper Press.

ONE who glances at the title-page of this little volume will naturally ask: "What is its object? Why should it be compiled at all?" Impertinent questions deserve no answer; and queries like these would be impertinent if made about a work in the ordinary course of literature, where an author's will is autocratic in conferring titles. But this diverges from that course in a manner which limits the editor's independence—to say nothing of autocracy. Thus the supposed questions, being natural, are pertinent; and, being pertinent, are to be answered.

The answer is not far to seek. Whatever else may follow, our primal object is to bring together from the many poems of a great author a few which are so marked by distinctive characteristics derived from the region of peculiar and intense individuality in which they were written, that they form a class by themselves. The purpose in annotating these poems is this: while most of them are now precious possessions of all English-speaking peoples, they were local in their inception and development. A description of the scenery which helped to inspire them, with a narration of the circumstances which led to their writing, and of those which attended their only public delivery in their author's living voice, may therefore enable the reader to enjoy, in addition to the inherent charms of the verse, something of that indescribable, and in a degree evanescent, sparkle and flavor which enchanted those who listened to its silver-toned enunciation fresh from the poet's heart and lips, while their own sympathies were attuned to harmony with what they heard by accompaniments that we shall endeavor to reproduce in such measure as we may.

If, in pursuing the purposes expressed, there shall seem to be a claim in behalf of the town of Pittsfield to some considerable share in the honor which attaches to every place and every institution with which the name of Oliver Wendell Holmes is in any way associated, we apprehend that the claim will be made good. The ardent expressions of his regard for the town, which we shall quote in the proper connections, will leave no doubt that if he could himself be conscious of such claim, he would fully approve it, imperfectly as it may be urged here; as, we believe, all who have a right to represent him will.

Liberal participation in the heritage of honor left by Dr. Holmes would be accorded to Pittsfield, even if her claim rested solely upon the basis that he wrote the beautiful poems in this collection under the influence of her scenery and of life associated with it, and that, before he committed them to the printer, he read them before large assemblages of her citizens and others gathered with them on grand public occasions. Something of this appears in the general collections of his works; but some of the verses inserted here are not included in those volumes; and others do not clearly indicate their birthplace. If, however, this were otherwise, it would not fully cover Pittsfield's claim upon the poet's memory. That rests upon a broader foundation, as we shall see.

Students of Dr. Holmes' works will observe that, in striking contrast with his other writings, there is in his Berkshire poems no allusion to scientific or classic lore, save a playful mention of the winged steed that he did not have, as he had swapped it away for a ploughman's horse. Nor is there much of the humor in which he excelled; although it laughs in two or three minor pieces, and pretty gayly in some prefatory speeches. But, for the most part, all is Nature; and Nature without scientific analysis, as she here spreads out her works for all who, like Dr. Holmes, have eyes to see; combined with the human sympathies which left nothing which pertained to humanity foreign to him. A terse writer of many true thoughts says: "Nature has no morbid strain." It is a sentiment that might have come from Dr. Holmes himself as a companion line to that in his Pittsfield Cemetery poem: "Cheerful Nature owns no mourning flower." He remembered both these traits in Nature's authorship when he made the translations of her works that his Berkshire poems essentially are. There is nothing in them either morbid or gloomy.

Said Jean Paul: "To describe any scene well, the poet must make the bosom of a man his *camera obscura*. Then will he see it poetically." Such a *camera* Dr. Holmes used in all his paintings of Berkshire scenery. And thus it was that the outcome of what he saw poetically was not reserved merely for lettered readers, but was freely mingled with the associated mental activities of men, whether that activity manifested itself in a body of farmers, the fraternal *alumni* of his *alma mater* or a whole organized community. But whether his verse was addressed to a learned, an unlearned, or a mixed auditory, his perfect accord with the harmonies of nature and his fine poetic sense, with his all controling pure taste, made it intelligible to and enjoyable by all.

Dr. Holmes had those rare intellectual gifts which, possessed as he possessed them, afford sure touchstones of genius: Capacity for great, beautiful, and true thought, with a faultless method of expressing it; both the thought and the expression of it being peculiar to himself; modeled upon no other author or school of authors; and transcending, not only the common level of authordom, but its elevations conspicuous enough to be observable. We speak of genius in the abstract, and perhaps have a fairly correct idea of it, as a congenital endowment of some few favored minds with powers, exceeding those of mere talent, for life-work to which it irresistibly impels them. But individual genius is unique, and therefore is to be studied individually. A clever biographer says: "The intellect of Holmes, though manifesting many strongly marked attributes, eludes all tests, preserves its individuality, and remains unclassified among original elements."

True; but it does not follow that the products of these attributes cannot be classified. Indeed they classify themselves. The genius of Dr. Holmes has many sides; and it is not for us to attempt an analysis even of that which was turned toward Berkshire. He, however, would be a singular reader, who should enjoy a favorite class of the poems of a favorite author for half a century without gaining some impression of what it was that charmed him.

In the light of such an impression, the ruling quality in Dr. Holmes' Berkshire poems is their entire naturalness. It is Nature herself that breathes through each and every line. While reading them we feel that what we enjoy was as much an "elixir of delight" for him when he received it from her as it is for us when we receive it from him. We need no analysis to assure us that it is the free uncontaminated outflow from a full and pure fountain, and not an indifferent stream from a force-pump.

And yet the genius of Dr. Holmes, as displayed in his Berkshire poems—which alone concern us here—had distinctive, although not obtrusively startling elements. They were very like the characteristics which a great critic ascribes admiringly to a German biographical writer whom he esteems of extraordinary merit. "The poet must express his inmost qualities in his verse; and the noblest poetry in all its varied but harmonious elements is the visible soul of the noblest man." And, with the slight modifications that we make, what Carlyle says of his admired author will apply equally well to the Berkshire poems of Dr. Holmes, and to himself as revealed in them. In style these poems are distinguished for clearness and grace of method, and for comprehensibility. In matter they point to an author of affectionate and exquisitely sympathetic nature; courteous but truthful; precise in expression; of quick apprehension; of just, extensive, often deep and fine, insight. This delineates very accurately the characteristics of Dr. Holmes in his relations to Berkshire as a poet. Nevertheless, coincidence with the intellectual constitution of Varnhagen von Ense does not in the least militate against the uniqueness of the American's genius; for in its processes and their fruit, the brain-work of the two men differed as essentially as biography differs from poetry.

It is no part of our purpose to attempt the slightest critical analysis of these Berkshire poems. Even could such an attempt succeed, the success would be out of all place here. The mourner might as well accompany the wreath he lays upon the tomb hallowed by affection, or the lover the bouquet he sends his mistress, with a botanical classification of its flowers.

That charm of poetry which penetrates all hearts open to the entrance of pure pleasures, and is enjoyed without conscious volition, is beyond analysis; and, even if some grim sage could resolve such subtile and ethereal joys into their ultimate elements, it would not enable him to reproduce the God-given odor of the rose or the inspired melody of the song, nor would his learned exposition add one whit to any soul's delight in them.

Every word in Dr. Holmes' verses has its meaning, and every sentence makes its impression. The meaning is clear and the impression is distinct—often incisive—without the aid of any interpreter; but those familiar with the scenes amid which, and the themes upon which, he wrote may recognize meanings and receive impressions hidden from readers not thus favored. To extend this familiarity more widely is the leading object of the annotation in this volume. We trust that it will not be looked upon as an attempt to gild refined gold; but rather with charitable eyes, as only an effort to expose a little more of it to view. Somebody has said that notes to a fine poem are like an anatomical lecture on a savory joint; but surely the most succulent and savory joint may be accompanied by condiments, provided that they develop, and do not mar or obscure, its native flavor. And any good housewife will tell us that some attention ought to be paid to the table on which it is served.

There is a side lesson taught by the wealth of poetry which this collection presents as the product of a brief interval of the poet's life. An old man in his moody moments, looking back over years which have vanished, leaving little to represent them, may be tempted to say with the Portuguese poet:

> What is life? A wild illusion,
> Fleeting shadow; fond delusion,
> Whose most steadfast substance seems
> But the dream of other dreams.

But one who has frequently to write even of commonplace lives and in the biographical-dictionary style, learns how much that is worth the doing is often scattered along very ordinary careers, often of much less than three-score years and ten. But when he contemplates the achievements, of deathless fame and priceless value, that were compressed into a fraction of Oliver Wendell Holmes' seven summers in Pittsfield, he is struck with amazement. The study affords a striking object-lesson for the young; for although powers of achievement like those of Dr. Holmes are rare, it is no reason, because our one, two, or three talents do not mount to the ten called genius, that they should be left to run to waste. They need the more cultivation.

And yet another ground for this compilation, if another is needed, will be found in the hope that it may render some of Pittsfield's own people more familiar with the poems comprised in it, and incidentally lead to a wider acquaintance with all the works of their author,—to the great advantage of their taste in literature, as well as in other matters. Nor will it be of small value, if, by giving any an intelligent and clear appreciation of the great poet's relations to their town, it shall at once strengthen and make more rational their pride in it. And Southey, in the passage from his "Doctor," which we have made our initial motto, shows that pride in one's own home-town is a most excellent thing to have, even if it leads to an estimate of its merits so undue and so disproportionate in comparison with the rest of the world, that it makes us appear rustic or provincial in cosmopolitan eyes.

And this brings us back to our primary motor: Pittsfield's home pride, and the justification of it by Dr. Holmes' legacy of honor, and otherwise.

Pittsfield, through the best representatives of its local pride, piques itself upon its completeness. Now, completeness is essentially different from perfection. Holy Scripture declares that "There is none perfect: no, not one." And he must indeed be "a blinded bigot" of a skeptic, who, living among men, disputes this averment, even if he denies its divine inspiration. There is no perfect man. To be sure, we do now and then, in biographical histories, or perhaps, at wide intervals, in living examples, come upon a tolerably complete man: one whose physical, intellectual, and moral natures all closely approximate perfection. But inevitably in some unguarded moment some little flaw or frailty betrays the infirmity of humanity even at its best. In the common mass of men, the perfection of an individual in one quality or in one ability is most often attained by the sacrifice of even moderate excellence in every other. We have somewhere read a story in which the scene was laid a couple of centuries, more or less, in the future, and in a country where triumphant socialism had subjected every thing to the control of a truly paternal government. Men and women were married, being officially paired after an official examination to determine their fitness for each other. The children born to this officially authorized union were trained by government officials for the special occupation and position in the world to which they had been officially assigned in babyhood, after a phrenological inspection—also official—to ascertain for what, in official opinion, wise Nature created each particular little one. Under this official process all the mental and physical faculties of a child which his officially predetermined station in life demanded were perfectly developed. All the rest dwindled to uselessness. Thus the fabled state had perfect blacksmiths and barristers, clergymen and carpenters, hair-dressers and hod-carriers, and so on to the end of the chapter; but not one single complete man.

Now, even as men are, so are the towns which they build, inhabit, and, for one reason or another, love and take pride in; that is, unless they are of the class without a tap-root, against whom Southey's "Doctor" sharply warns us. There may be towns and cities in which a too predominant devotion to one pursuit in life has had an effect similar to that of the ideal development and repression of each individual's natural faculties which our story-teller paints as the logical outcome of socialist theories of government. These, however, are rare exceptions. Either from natural advantages, well-directed public spirit, personal enterprise and liberality, or a confluence of streams from several of these fountain-heads of prosperity and excellence, most American towns come reasonably near to perfection in more than one or two of the elements which, if all were present in like degree, would constitute what might be properly called completeness: that is, a complete circle of those elements, such as manufactures and commerce, with the means and the spirit to advance them; healthfulness with the best sanitary provisions to retain it; a cultivated community, with schools, libraries, and other facilities for, and incitements to, further culture; religious institutions adapted to varying creeds and forms of worship; noble and beautiful scenery; with whatever else is needful to invite and satisfy permanent or alternate residents, as well as those who seek a brief resort for health or pleasure.

What those uncompromising representatives and champions of Pittsfield's pride, we spoke of awhile ago, claim and pique themselves upon in behalf of their idolized town is this, that in it the circle of these widely varied elements of completeness, and of others cognate to them, is, without exception, complete: not that each or any of them is complete or perfect in itself; but that the good town is distinguished by a fairly close approach to perfection in each and is steadily advancing toward it in all where Nature admits advance.

Philosophic Thomas Carlyle makes an assertion concerning the building of men's habitations that affords a parallel to the Scriptural apothegm regarding their own moral and intellectual structure. "Perfection," he avers, "is unattainable. No carpenter in the world ever made a mathematically accurate right-angle;

yet all carpenters know when it is right enough; and do not botch their work and lose their wages by making it too right." Still there are many right-angles in the framework of a house, and if most of them do not closely approximate mathematical accuracy, it will never come to completion. Doubtless what Mr. Carlyle means is a legal maxim slightly varied: *De minimis lex naturæ non curatur*—The law of nature does not concern itself about trifles. Nor should men trouble themselves about trifling errors in their own work. Nevertheless even approximate perfection is not likely to be attained in a structure of any kind unless the absolute is kept in view: and much less if it is deliberately thrust out of sight. Strive as we may, there is no danger of getting near enough to perfection to "botch our work."

The structure of a town is very like that of a man. It has, or should have, body, mind, and soul; and each of these distinct components needs cultivation. So long as a just balance is reserved, we need not fear that either will get too much of it. There will always be room for more. Better so: Who but a drone would wish to live in a place where there is no call for effort, or even strife, to make it better? It would be insufferably dull.

Town? city? country? Call Pittsfield which you will; for us, it is the same old long-loved town. A city charter does not change its nature. The greater portion of its territory still remains quite as fit for a quiet, secluded country home as any rural region whatever; while almost all the rest is a striking example of the *rus in urbe*, country and city interpenetrating each other. We think that, on the whole, we will keep to the stalwart old New England word, town; under which Pittsfield, like so many of her sister Massachusetts municipalities —and conspicuously among them—has, in one way or another, won so much honor that it may rightfully be called glory.

But to return: There is one element in Pittsfield's circle of completeness which our uncompromising ultraists will not, under any compulsion, admit to fall one little iota short of absolute perfection. This is her scenery, which, they insist, lacks literally nothing that inland landscape can have to make it altogether enchanting. This is a trifle extravagant. Very critical eyes — even if not hypercritical or sharpened by jealousy as our enthusiasts would be likely to charge—very critical eyes may by close scrutiny detect here and there a blot, to sustain Carlyle's dictum of the impossible, even when applied to the wealth of color, grace, and grandeur that enriches the valley here embosomed among the symmetrical dome-crowned hills of Berkshire. And yet this extravagant claim is so plausibly and pleasantly like truth that an observer at all sensitive to Nature's loveliness will find it in his heart rather to sympathize with than harshly to utterly reject it: especially if his visit shall happen on one of those glorious summer or autumn days, when the foam on the waterfalls, bound though they be in servitude to mill-wheels, is "excellently bright," and the hillside denudings of the coal-burner's ax, though rough as his unshaven face, are encircled with undulating curves of a livelier, richer verdure than that of the surrounding unbroken foliage; curves that often, on a November or December night, are transformed into serpentine borders of living fire, as the dry brushwood, heaped along the edges of the rude openings, is set aflame by a chance spark or by a woodman's match.

But let pass perfection. What have we, imperfect mortals, to do with it anyhow? Pittsfield's scenery is at least quite good enough for the best of us; and the best of us best appreciate and enjoy it. To its thus appreciatively enjoyed charms, the town's parks and its broad streets, park-like by virtue of their wide fringes of grass-carpeted courtyards, and their noble colonnades of overhanging elms and maples, contribute not a little; but very much more is due to its magnificent outlook in every direction, to a boundary of mountain ranges surpassed by none in their grace of contour and the majesty of their grand curvilinear sweep around the horizon. Standing on any considerable elevation near the main streets, such as the platform-roof of the Academy of Music or the tower of the Maplewood Gymnasium, the spectator finds himself, more than a thousand feet above the sea level, in the center of an elliptical valley fifty miles long, with the proportions in area which architects love to give their choicest structures, while the symmetry with which point answers to opposing point exceeds the attainment of art. Within its green and graceful encircling walls lies cradled a rolling country of minor hills and valleys; with, here and there, a fertile plain. A hundred lakelets, mostly in the low lands, but sometimes on the very hill-tops, dot the wide landscape with the gleam of their dimpling waters; while frequent towns, villages, fine farm-houses, and not a few costly country-seats endow it with human life. Through this superb upland valley flows, renowned in song and story, the " blue, winding Housatonic;" receiving in its myriad graceful meanders the silvery tribute of unnumbered rills and streamlets. Upon this vision of beauty looks down, from the northernmost border of Massachusetts, Greylock, its loftiest summit, in more than mountain majesty — often of a summer morning, "cloud-girdled on his purple throne;" adding grandeur to grace.

Of course all this is not visible to our spectator in every detail; but what he does see will enable him to comprehend the whole. And what he will note as a pleasant peculiarity is that, multitudinous as the mountains are around him, not one is oppressively near.

Features like these, thus combined, go far toward constituting perfect scenery; and, admitting the impossibility of perfections, let it also be admitted that this "borders on the impossible." If, however, Pittsfield scenery had been undeniably perfect and complete in all that meets the eye, those who are now its most loyal and ardent worshipers would have been first to acknowledge that something was yet lacking, had there not been associated with it a record of heroic and patriotic men and deeds; and had it not received a soul from the living and loving presence of men and women of genius, and the magic touch of their pens. Without such accessories no affluence of Nature's loveliness suffices a landscape. We need not recount the town's brave and patriotic action from its earliest to its latest days, whenever the country's peril has called for it, nor recall the names of the patriots and heroes who have given luster to its annals. Enough of both for our present purpose is embalmed in the country's history. Nor should we speak specifically of the men and women of letters who have helped to give it character and fame, were it not that comparatively few readers are familiar with literary biographical history; and did not what we shall say lead up to and illustrate our ultimate subject. As it is, we shall confine ourselves to little more than cursory mention of a very few of the very many whose mere names would call up charmed thoughts for cultured loiterers along the delightful avenues that, branching in every direction from Pittsfield's beautiful and historic little central park, stretch away into regions of ever-varying landscape, revealing at every turn what poetic Governor Andrew so happily termed "the delicious surprises of Berkshire."

There is a kind of commonplace people who have an unaccountable but inveterate hankering to get where commonplace people are out of place. Their most preposterous, but seemingly irresistible proclivity is, to inflict names as commonplace as they can pick out from their commonplace observation upon localities, and whatever else is as far from commonplace, as the commonplace very often is from common-sense. It is not much to the credit of a community with plenty of good taste that its listless indifference often permits this unhappy craze to have its wicked way: for it is wicked to soil with stupidity what Nature has made beautiful and genius has hallowed. But such soiling is permitted. And thus it happened that one of the most superb avenues which entice the lover of Nature's loveliness into the romantic regions around—and one with the proudest associations—became "Middle Street," for the, to a commonplace mind, good and sufficient reason that it is, beyond all question, the middle road of three between Pittsfield and Lenox.

This avenue affords a superb "drive," commanding broad and noble views of mountains, hills, and valleys, and of the Housatonic River, which it crosses. The same, excepting the river, is, however, true of all Pittsfield, and of most Berkshire roads. But this Middle Street —which, thanks to some reformers of taste, we shall not be again forced to call by that stupid name—this Middle Street—this *ci-devant* Middle Street somewhat excels all its rivals in some regards of which commonplace people know little, comprehend less, and care not at all. There are pleasant, patriotic, quaint, curious, and romantic traditions associated with one or another of all these rides and walks; but this middle road to Lenox has the advantage in this, that it was the earliest highway in the township; being part of the first which crossed Berkshire from the Connecticut boundary-line on the south to that of Vermont on the north. Even before the coming of the white man the Mohegans had a trail nearly coincident with it, and more of their relics have been found in its vicinity than in any other section of Pittsfield. It must also have been the pathway of the early settlers from the Connecticut valley; and the magnates among them clustered so thickly in its neighborhood as to make it out of question the court end of the young town. Here and now, however, its predominant interest for us lies in the fact that on it was the summer-home of Oliver Wendell Holmes and that of his ancestors for three generations before him. Of this we shall have occasion to speak more at large in another connection. It is sufficient to say here that the death of Dr. Holmes revived attention to these facts; intensifying the repugnance to the insipidity of the old name in the minds of citizens of culture and influence, at whose instance the City Council changed it to Holmes Road. And Holmes Road it will be while Pittsfield streets have names: adding, by the associations which it will recall, a new charm to an already charming region; and giving the city a new memorial of the poet's life in it.

But let us resume our purpose of citing a few examples of authors, besides Dr. Holmes, distinguished in the higher walks of literary composition and eloquent utterance, who have helped to invest Pittsfield with interest for the admirers of genius and the lovers of literature. Naturally the first which comes to mind is Dr. Holmes' nearest neighbor, of the guild of letters—Herman Melville. A gentle elevation on the west side of Holmes Road, a few rods south of its namesake's summer villa, is crowned by a spacious, old-fashioned gambrel-roofed mansion, rich in the memories of more than a century. Mr. Melville must have known it well in his youth, when he was in the family of his uncle, Major Thomas Melville, in the still more historic old mansion now known as Broadhall; and was master of a district school so located that his nearest way to it was through the farm attached to the gambrel-roofed house of Holmes Road. In 1848, shortly after his marriage, and the brilliant success of his first books, "Omoo" and "Typee," he passed the summer in the same old broad-halled mansion,* which

---

*In calling this old mansion "Broadhall" here and elsewhere, we deliberately, for the sake of convenience and intelligibility, commit an anachronism, rather than change the name with every change of owners, which is the country wont. It was named some three years after Melville, Longfellow, and ex-President Tyler were boarders in it; and in this wise: It had then become the residence of Mr. J. R. Morewood, and at a little party in its parlors—not by any means "all silent," it was declared that a mansion with so much character

was then a boarding-house, where, among other agreeable fellow-boarders, he found the poet Longfellow with his wife and children. This summer at Broadhall reviving his acquaintance, with its neighbor, the old farm-house of Holmes Road, he bought it, and it was his well-loved home for many years. He named the place " Arrowhead;" having, in his first plowing of its fields, turned up one of " the pointed flints that left the fatal bow" of the Mohegan warrior or hunter. He found the mansion a spacious gambrel-roofed house of two stories; he made it a house of many stories; writing in it almost all his later works. Among these the most locally interesting, though far from the most widely known, is the " Piazza Tales;" so titled because its stories were built upon a piazza which he added to the north end of the house where it overlooks a noble landscape, extending through a picturesque vista of twenty miles,

---

ought to have a significant name. The selection of one from the variety proposed was left to chance. Each proposer wrote his proposed name on a slip of paper and dropped it in a basket; the first drawn from it, to be accepted. This chanced to be "Broadhall," which was written by Herman Melville. The selection was so "pat" that it was hailed with unanimous approval; although some serious, or rather merry, suspicion was expressed that chance—lest she might prove Miss Chance —had a judicious adviser in the person of some one of the ladies of the mansion.

to Greylock,—to Greylock, ever companionably present in Berkshire, whatever miles may intervene. A New England farm-house so venerable as that at Arrowhead could not fail of its huge old elephantine chimney; and Mr. Melville made it the hero of one of his most curious and characteristic sketches, " My Chimney and I." He regarded it as the overbearing tyrant of his home, as he, himself, very decidedly was not.

Mr. Melville was extravagantly fond of excursions among the Berkshire hills and valleys; a well-preserved relic of his early passion for far wider wanderings. His rambles were never solitary, and rarely with a single companion unless they involved more than one day's tramp on foot. He rather delighted to lead parties of kindred tastes; often including guests of note from abroad, and always some ladies of his own and intimately friendly families. In such fellowship he climbed to every alluring hill-top, and explored every picturesque corner and hidden nook that he could hear of, or find by seeking. Picnic revelers may be sure that whatever romantic camping-ground they choose in Berkshire, Herman Melville has been there before them, and that its echoes have rung with the laughter and the merry shouts of his rollicking followers. From many of these resorts he drew pictures for his tales; among others, from Balance Rock, Potter Mountain—a favorite with him—and the grand rounded summit—about two miles southwest from his residence and from that of Dr. Holmes—which he named October Mountain for the gorgeousness of its autumn tints.

An incident of singular interest marked one of his excursions; and though it happened between Stockbridge and Great Barrington, it will bring us back to Holmes Road. We constantly need something to bring us back from the wanderings to which we are enticed by Berkshire's beauties.

In 1849, Nathaniel Hawthorne came to live awhile in the little red cottage, which he made famous, on the border of the Stockbridge Bowl —the Sedgwick-Sigourney name for what the learned map-makers call Lake Mahekanituck— some seven miles south of Arrowhead. Melville had written for *The New York Literary World*, edited by his friends the brothers Duyckinck, a most appreciative and singularly sympathetic review of "The Scarlet Letter." This article was not only appreciative of, but appreciated by, Hawthorne. Yet when the two authors came to be neighbors, as neighborhood is reckoned in the country, there was at first a certain shyness in their intercourse; probably from the fear of each lest he should seem to the other to presume too much upon what he had said and done. It was a sensitiveness natural to the pride of genius; but so shadowy and irksome a barrier could not long keep apart men so formed for fellowship. It was broken down during an excursion when the two were driven by a sudden, severe, and prolonged summer shower to take refuge together in a narrow recess on the west side of Bryant's Monument Mountain. There, undisturbed by the tumult of the elements, the two great original thinkers and writers, neither of them "made altogether by the common pattern," learned to know each other; mind to mind and heart to heart. Thenceforward their friendship was that of kindred though diverse intellects; and of faith and feeling in which they were not diverse.

The intercourse thus founded extended to the families of the two friends. Hawthorne's biographer tells us that when Melville was approaching the cottage by the lake, a joyous shout went up: "Here comes Typee!" the pet name they had given him. With Mr. Melville's free, hearty, and jovial, although always highbred and dignified, manner, this might have been expected; but Mr. Hawthorne, also, could throw off his reserve for a roll and a frolic with children; and he was as welcome at Arrowhead as Melville was at the lakeside. It is not this chiefly, however, that brings us back to Holmes

Road. As we learn from the same biographer, one who passed over it in 1849-50 might sometimes have enjoyed a rare spectacle. If it chanced to be in summer or early autumn, the great barn-doors of the Arrowhead barn would have been wide open, and if he cast a glance within he might have seen the two friends, reclining on piles of fragrant new-mown hay, and basking in the genial in-pouring rays of the sun, while they held high converse on the mysteries and revelations of the world and those who people it.

We pass from Holmes Road, the Canoe Meadows, Arrowhead, and their memories, to courtly East Street, Elm Knoll and the "House of the Old Clock on the Stairs;" with the memories they recall.

The story which locates in "the old-fashioned country-seat" of Elm Knoll the ancient timepiece celebrated in Longfellow's exquisite poem has been so often told that it almost seems trite; and yet a brief, exact restatement may please many readers of the soulful verses.

Very early in the century now drawing to a close, the old mansion, even then not unstoried, became the residence of Thomas Gold, a lawyer of some note, and a man of wealth as wealth was then counted in Berkshire. His daughter, Maria Theresa, became the wife of Hon. Nathan Appleton, a Boston gentleman of culture and distinction. After Mr. Gold's death, the homestead, although the property and home of his widow while she lived, was the summer residence of the Appleton family. Mrs. Gold, like all the ladies of the Gold-Appleton connection, was remarkable for dignity, grace, and kindliness of manner. Her intellectual character, based on good native abilities, the best home education the country then afforded, and the highest principles, had been broadened and refined by European travel. Her relations with the Appleton family must have been most agreeable.

After a most romantic wooing, the poet Longfellow "won the heart and hand" of Nathan Appleton's daughter, Frances Elizabeth; as one of Mr. Longfellow's biographers states, "while she was spending a summer in Pittsfield." We are not quite sure of that. But, at any rate, they were married at Boston, July 13, 1843, and the last and longest of their three wedding tours was to visit the bride's relatives and friends in Pittsfield, where they lingered until late in August. Then the poet first saw the old clock at the head of the broad flight of stairs leading from the spacious entrance-hall of the Gold-Appleton mansion. He did not, however, begin to write the poem which has made it famous until November 12, 1845, when its memory was recalled by a passage in the

HENRY W. LONGFELLOW
In 1844.

writings of Bridaine, an old French missionary; which also furnished the refrain, "Forever, never! Never, forever"—"*Toujours, jamais! Jamais, toujours!*" The poem at once attained remarkable popularity, which half a century has increased rather than diminished. And the frequent allusions to it in its author's diary show that it was as much a favorite with him as it was with his readers. The marvelous hold which it took upon multitudes of hearts is explained by the elements of deep thought and feeling which combine in it. The refrain suggests and almost expresses the emotions that spring irrepressibly while contemplating a timepiece of past fashion, that has marked the hours as they grew to years, and the years as they grew to generations in an old family mansion. Consonant with this voice from the dial is the story, which the poet makes the ancient timepiece tell, of life and of death in that mansion. This story has its counterpart in mansion homes all over the country and in all countries of mansion homes. Nay; in all essential particulars, in cottage homes as well. The poet painted his passing scenes not only vividly, but "using the bosom of a man as his *camera obscura;*" and the result was what always happens when poets like Holmes and Longfellow adopt the practice commended by Jean Paul. Mr. Longfellow must himself have felt that he had celebrated the mansion as much at least as the clock on its stairs; for, it will be observed that in his diary he rarely speaks of the old clock simply, but almost invariably of the "House of the Old Clock." The clock was of the tall old-fashioned kind made in Pittsfield and Lanesboro, late in the last century and early in the present. In old Berkshire families they are preserved as precious heirlooms, while strangers buy them at high prices merely as "antiques." That which Longfellow saw in

> "The old-fashioned country seat,
> Somewhat back from the village street,"

and made eloquent on its rostrum there, was, some years ago, called to Boston, where it stands in the hallway of the Appleton mansion. Professor Longfellow placed one of the same class in the hall of the Craigie House, his Cambridge residence, where many visitors erroneously supposed it to be the original clock of the poem.

Mr. Longfellow's wedding visit to Pittsfield was followed by others. The most interesting was in the summer of 1849, which he spent at the Broadhall boarding-house. He was much impressed by the beauty of the neighboring South Mountain, and the variety of grand views from it. He took great pleasure with his children on the shores of the charming lakelet in the Broadhall grounds, where he one day had an adventure, with danger enough to give it zest. The little ones craved some beautiful pond-lilies that floated on the surface of the lakelet—to which some of the later ladies of Broadhall gave the pet name of "The Lily-Bowl." There was no craft near, save a crazy, leaky little boat; but, like the devoted father and child-lover he was, he risked himself in it to secure the coveted prize, although the miserable little broken shell threatened every moment to sink with him. He tells of several pleasant drives, but was clearly the most delighted with an afternoon excursion to Roaring Brook. This notable mountain streamlet dashes down a romantic gorge in the west side of Washington Mountain,—a summit of the Hoosacs a couple of miles southwest of Dr. Holmes' villa. Mr. Longfellow visited it one summer day and gives the following spirited account of the excursion and word-painting of the brook and gorge in his diary:

August 28th.—In the morning, sat with the children by the water-wheel in the brook, then walked to the village, for carriage to take us in the afternoon to Roaring Brook. A lovely drive, and lovelier walk. Leaving the carriage at the foot of the hill, we climbed the rough wagon-way along the borders of the brook, catching glimpses of its waterfalls through the woods, and hearing the perpetual music of its murmur. The water is of a lively brown color, like Rhenish wine—the Olympian wine spilled from the goblet of Hebe when she fell. We climbed as far as the mill—a saw-mill, bringing to mind the little poem translated from the German by Bryant."

At the time of this excursion, Longfellow was writing his novel "Kavanagh"—an enchanting little volume for readers of dainty taste and thought—and he painted his visit into it in glowing colors. George Lowell Austin, in his "Life, Works and Friendships of Longfellow," says: "The tale was written in the Melville House [Broadhall—ED.] not far from the Pittsfield home of Dr. Holmes. Most of the scenery and a little of the story was derived from his wooing and marriage." The paragraph regarding the Roaring Brook is as follows:

"Every State, and almost every county of New England has its Roaring Brook—a mountain streamlet, overhung by woods, impeded by a mill, encumbered by fallen trees; but ever-rushing, racing, roaring down, through gurgling gullies and filling the forest with its delicious sound and freshness: the drinking-places of home-returning herds; the mysterious haunts of squirrels and blue-jays; the sylvan retreat of schoolboys, who frequent it in summer holidays and mingle their restless thoughts with its restless, exuberant, and rejoicing stream."

Longfellow was not the only guest of the House of the Old Clock who left choice memories behind. In Mr. Appleton's time many such enjoyed its hospitality. Of these Charles Sumner has for us the deepest interest. In the late summer of 1844, he was slowly recovering from an alarming illness, and his physician advised him that Berkshire air would greatly hasten and confirm his convalescence. He was a great favorite with the Appleton family, and one of Longfellow's dearest friends, having been groomsman at his wedding with Miss Appleton a year before. He was therefore invited to make their country-seat his home as long as he would, and, accepting the invitation, he became their guest for several weeks. His visit delighted him and his recovery was rapid. There was one circumstance which contributed materially to his enjoyment, which will also contribute materially to the testimony we are accumulating from the most widely informed and fastidious witnesses to the summer loveliness of the region around Dr. Holmes' summer home.

Hon. Edward A. Newton, a friend and neighbor of the Appletons, and a man quick to perceive and appreciate intellectual qualities like those of their guest, loaned him a fine saddle-horse, enabling him to make frequent excursions over the avenues we have described; whose attractions he very warmly acknowledged. But he very soon had companionship which doubled their charms. Twelve years before—in 1832—when he was a law-student at Cambridge, he became thoroughly fascinated with the beauty and genius of Fanny Kemble, who, then twenty-one years old—was making an American theatrical tour with her father. His personal acquaintance with her was, however, of the slightest, until he came to Berkshire. Naturally his first ride after getting settled in his Pittsfield resting-place was to visit his old bosom friends the Sedgwicks at Lenox; and, with them, he found the lady of his old admiration, a dear, valued, and honored guest. It was a delightful surprise.

Both had known much of life's changes in the interval between 1832 and 1844. Mr. Sumner, with a ripening intellect and a personnel vastly improved from that of the rather uncouth youth of his student life, had become a favorite in society, and had won a wider than national reputation as a writer upon law. Miss Kemble had become Mrs. Pierce Butler, and had suffered much in the unhappy marriage which was dissolved the next year. Each was now thirty-three years old; of an age and with the finest capacities for the keenest enjoyment of noble scenery and the highest order of conversational intercourse. Neither was without sorrow; but neither would submit to conquest by it.

This combination of circumstances more than revived Mr. Sumner's fascination with the lady whose genius he had early learned to appreciate; and she could not fail to be gratified by and reciprocate the admiration of a man whose opinions were authority in the highest intellectual circles of America, and were respected in corresponding circles of English life. That she did so, is proved by many expressions in her published writings, as well as by her conduct. Mr. Sumner's feeling toward her is illustrated by a passage in one of his letters. She had introduced the English sport of archery into Lenox summer-life, where we believe it still flourishes. Having written of a jolting ride with "Sam" Ward, one day, he continues: "Afterward we looked on while, in a field not far-off, the girls and others were engaged in the sport of archery. Mrs. Butler hit the target in the golden middle." Her triumph evidently pleased him.

In another letter he writes: "I count much upon the readings from Shakespeare, the conversations and society of Fanny Kemble" (He restores here her maiden name), "who has promised to ride with me, and introduce me to the beautiful lanes and wild paths of these mountains. She seems a noble woman—peculiar, bold, masculine, and unaccommodating; but having a burning sympathy with all that is high, true, and humane."

The next day he wrote to his friend George S. Hillard, who accompained him to Pittsfield, but had returned: "I wish you were still here. Your presence would help me bear the weight of Fanny Kemble's conversation; for much as I admire her, I confess to a certain awe and sense of her superiority which makes me at times anxious to subside into my own inferiority and leave the conversation to other minds."

Here is an account of a Sunday visit to Lenox:

"I was perplexed whether to use Mr. Newton's horse, as I presumed his owner never used him on Sunday, but my scruples gave way before my longing for the best of exercises. I left Pittsfield as the first bell tolled for church and reached Lenox some time before the second bell. I sat in Mrs. [Charles] Sedgwick's room; the time passed on. Mrs. Butler joined us; again time passed on. Mrs. Butler proposed to accompany me back to Pittsfield on horseback. I stayed to the cold dinner, making it lunch; again time passed on from delay in saddling the horses. We rode the longest way, and I enjoyed my companion much."

The longest way was by the east road. which

runs along the base of October Mountain, crossing Roaring Brook and the Housatonic River, whose serpentine course is here seen to great advantage.

Toward the end of summer, Mr. Sumner wrote to Dr. Howe: "Hillard is here with me, and my situation is made most agreeable by the kindest hospitality. We took a drive the first day, to Lenox, where the Sedgwicks received me warmly,—somewhat as one risen from the dead. Next day, we made an excursion to Lanesboro, enjoying much the meadows, green fields, rich country, and beautiful scenery. I shall linger here another week." Accepting an invitation in this letter, Dr. Howe made a brief visit to the "House of the Old Clock." After his return Mr. Sumner wrote him on September 8: "Since you were here I have waxed in strength most visibly. To-day I rode two hours as the escort of two damsels of the place; one of them, the governor's daughter. Dr. Robert Campbell, a most respectable physician of the place, called a few evenings since. He found my pulse 112, and said that its derangement was difficult to explain. He since met me in the street and volunteered to say that he had thought a great deal of my case, and was convinced that the derangement of my pulse was not to be referred to any organic disease, but to some affection of the nerves; which is precisely my version of it. I am doing so well here, making such palpable progress, and friends are so kind, that I shall linger in Pittsfield or Lenox the greater part—perhaps all of next week; when I shall be very strong.

Mr. Sumner's sanguine anticipations of restoration to perfect and permanent health by the aid of Berkshire air were fully realized; although something of the credit may be claimed for the very agreeable—not to say enchanting—circumstances under which he breathed it. This pleasant and interesting episode in the earlier life of the great orator and statesman is also a pleasant and interesting episode in the story of Pittsfield and Lenox life. We present the pictures of his rides and walks with the great actress and woman of genius, as charms wherewith those who follow in the scenes which delighted them may conjure up fantasies of delight for themselves.

Longfellow fully shared Sumner's admiration for Fanny Kemble; and in neither did it fade with time. Both were in raptures with her Shakespearian readings. After one at Boston, in 1849, when Longfellow had recently returned from Pittsfield and Mrs. Kemble from Lenox, he wrote her a sonnet complimenting it as it deserved. "It pleased her much," and Sumner copied it for publication in the *Evening Transcript:* a pretty little incident of the beautiful friendships of the little group of great minds to which the poet and the orator belonged.

In 1853 Nathan Appleton sold the House of the Old Clock to Thomas F. Plunkett, who made it his residence. But the "free-hearted hospitality" that "used to be," continued to be, and was enjoyed by the same class of guests. We can, however, mention only one; Dr. Josiah Gilbert Holland, editor, essayist, novelist, poet, and historian, who was for many years in many ways associated with Pittsfield from the time when he was a student in its medical college; and whose careful and most appreciative biography was written by Mrs. H. M. Plunkett, the present mistress of the "Old House" of many memories.

We may seem to have wandered far from our asserted theme; but we wish to remind the reader that the region which Dr. Holmes loved so well, and honored so much, that it can almost be called his own, had charms for other like minds. We would avoid leaving the impression that he was for Pittsfield the lone swallow that does not make a summer, whereas he was in fact the most tuneful, the most loving, and the most nearly native of many summer song-birds who have loved its haunts and left them melodious with the echoes of their praise: foremost also among the men of genius whose fame, mingling with the glory of its scenery, imparts to it a richer tinge.

"I hope there will be luster enough in one or more of the names with which I shall gild my pages to redeem the dullness of all that is merely personal in my recollections." Dr. Holmes printed this in the introduction to one of his books. We have carefully examined the volume in question; and there is not in it the slightest particle of dullness to be redeemed. The sentence quoted is therefore entirely superfluous. Being utterly useless to its author, and exactly adapted to our needs, we shall appropriate and adopt it without scruple. By the way, it was quite a habit of Dr. Holmes to write that which his readers wished they had written themselves; it being just what they thought they had thought before.

Dr. Holmes' verse, both in its sentiments and in his generous contributions of it to the town's great intellectual festivals, shows clearly his warm regard for Pittsfield; but yet stronger evidence that his love for the place was genuine and deep, is found in his private correspondence and public prose utterances. Of these we shall present some glowing words in their natural connections; but will here content ourselves with a single letter. It is not more emphatic or explicit than those to be quoted later; but we give it place here because it states concisely some points which introduce the writer as a Berkshire man, and prepare the way for much that is to follow. Dr. Holmes once said in Pittsfield that he was so fond of newspaper reading that he was obliged to systematically restrict himself to a limited number in each class that he cared for. It was another proof of his kindly sympathies with our common humanity. It will be observed that, except "The Vision of the Housatonic River," every one of the poems in the present collection was first printed in a Pittsfield newspaper. This, to be sure, was because they were included in reports of public occasions. Still as their author expressed surprise and pleasure on account of the accuracy of the work, the representatives of the local press will be apt to remember it. The letter which we quote was addressed to the Berkshire Press Club, declining an invitation to its annual dinner in 1880. It is a good example of the courtesy with which Dr. Holmes uniformly softened such declinations when compelled to make them. Still his uniform utterances at every opportunity leave no doubt of the sincerity of what he wrote as to his relations with Pittsfield.

"BOSTON, Oct. 16, 1880.

"GENTLEMEN:—I thank you for your very kind invitation to enjoy a social evening with the Berkshire editors and reporters. Seven of the happiest summers of my life were passed in Berkshire with the Housatonic running through my meadows and Greylock looking into my study windows. It pleases me to know that I am not wholly forgotten in the flourishing town and almost city of Pittsfield, to which my great-grandfather (Col. Jacob Wendell) rode, on horseback through the woods, when it was an Indian settlement or camp.

"I regret very much that it is not in my power to be with you at the American House; but no outside guest can be missed at a meeting enlivened by the wit and talent sure to be seated at a board surrounded by editors and reporters.

"I am, etc.,
"O. W. HOLMES."

II.

BERKSHIRE JUBILEE SPEECH AND POEM.

Sketch of the Jubilee—The Dinner—David Dudley Field's Journey of a Day—Catherine Sedgwick's Chronicles—Dr. Holmes' Table Speech—His Poem of Welcome.

SOMETHING of Oliver Wendell Holmes' relation to Pittsfield and Berkshire is intimated in the letter with which our prologue closes; but his affiliation with the town will appear more definitely as we proceed; still using his own words as a basis and guide. And we begin with those spoken at the Berkshire Jubilee of 1844. The Berkshire Jubilee:—Fifty years ago that name would have needed no interpretation in a connection like this. The unique character of the festival, the many famous participants in it, and the great number of the mountain county's sons and daughters who flocked to it from homes in all sections of the Union, secured liberal reports of, and comments upon, its proceedings in all considerable American journals. But all things are food for edacious Time; and even a little half-century is a ravenous devourer of newspaper fame. The story of the Jubilee is still locally extant; but even at home, although a little revived by the recurrence of its fiftieth anniversary, it begins to take on the phantom-like obscurity of tradition. Elsewhere, now and then, a minute biographer alludes to it in his memoir of some prominent actor in it; taking good care to provide an explanatory foot-note, or its equivalent. Yet it was a right memorable occasion; and one that deserves a permanent record. That its name and some hint of its character will be preserved is made sure by the inclusion of Dr. Holmes' poem of welcome to it in the permanent collection of his works; but even there it calls for the annotation we are to give it here.

THE JUBILEE.

For some years previous to 1844, Rev. Russell S. Cook, of New York, a native of New Marlboro, a resident of Lenox in his youth, and a frequent loving visitor to it in his mature life, was secretary of the American Tract Society. His official duties called him to all sections of the country; and everywhere he found Berkshire men in respectable, and often in high, positions. Impressed by the spontaneous expressions of warm regard for their old mountain homes by those whom he earliest met, further inquiry wherever he went convinced him that this feeling was uniform and universal.

From these and cognate observations, Mr. Cook conceived the idea of bringing these emigrants together in a social reunion at some convenient central point in Berkshire, with a view to forming a band of union among them; awakening in the citizens of the county an interest in the fame and usefulness of those who had gone out from among them, and also of furnishing to the world an illustration of the influence New England was having in the formation of the character of the country. Mr. Cook suggested this idea from time to time in his official visits, and found it everywhere cordially approved; but its realization was postponed, awaiting the recovery of the country from the financial depression of 1837; and probably, also, the completion of the Western (now the Boston and Albany) Railroad to Pittsfield, which did not happen until the late fall of 1842. In the spring of 1843, Mr. Cook, incidentally meeting Judge Joshua A. Spencer, of Utica, a native of Great Barrington, broached the subject to him. The judge heartily concurred in his idea, and the two gentlemen agreed upon a plan which was afterward substantially carried out. Both were men of influence personally, as well as from their official positions. Leading New York newspapers gave their earnest assistance, the name "Berkshire Jubilee" being first printed in the *Journal of Commerce*, whose editor, Colonel Stone, was foremost in his helpfulness. There was no difficulty in organizing a "New York Committee" zealous for the proposed reunion, with names upon it fit to conjure with: such as William Cullen Bryant, Orville Dewey, Judge Samuel R. Betts, David Dudley Field, Theodore Sedgwick, Marshall S. Bidwell, and Drake Mills. This committee communicated with gentlemen in Pittsfield, where, and in the county, committees were formed for the local work.

Then all went swimmingly. It was determined to hold the Jubilee at Pittsfield, August 22 and 23, 1844. The program called for a sermon and historical poem on the first day, an oration in the forenoon and a dinner in the afternoon of the second: all preceded by formal and informal welcomes and greetings, which proved to be warm and heartfelt, and interspersed with poems, hymns, and other minor exercises, some of which were of very marked character; such as an essay upon the then recently deceased William Ellery Channing by his friend Miss Sedgwick, and an ode on Berkshire by Mrs. Frances Ann (Fanny) Kemble.

Near the Pittsfield Union Railroad passenger station—which indeed stands on the edge of its southern slope—there rises the most conspicuous natural elevation in the township, save its very narrow mountain borders. It is almost two hundred rods long and forty wide, and its summit is about sixty feet above the mean level of the city streets. It was originally the farm of Dr. Timothy Childs, one of the most honored of Pittsfield's Revolutionary patriots; and, although it is now covered with fine streets and avenues, in 1844 there was no house upon it except the homestead which he built, and in his lifetime occupied. Thus it commanded an entirely unobstructed view of the noble valley, with ever-majestic Greylock looking down upon it from the north, and the graceful triune Lenox Range, with Yocun's Seat, its loftiest peak, not far away on the south. The Housatonic flowed along its western base, and the village lay smiling on the east.

All its memories and features marked this fair hill as the proper spot for most of the exercises of the Jubilee; and a platform was erected near the southern extremity of its summit upon which it was planned to conduct all, except the receptions and the dinner. But, when the people had assembled for the sermon, a violent rain-storm drove them, "in most admired disorder," from the hill to the time-honored, fairly handsome and spacious Congregational church. There the sermon was preached by that most eminent educator, metaphysician, and pulpit orator, President Mark Hopkins of Williams College. Dr. Hopkins has been happily characterized as "massive-minded;" and his Jubilee sermon was what was to be expected from such a preacher. But he was also a true son of one of the most Berkshire of all old Berkshire families. He dearly loved the scenery which had delighted him from childhood, and he was proud of the history in whose glories he had good right to share. He knew well how to prize all that went to make up the grand mountain-walled individuality which peculiarly characterizes the county. Naturally inspired by an occasion which kindled and concentrated thought of all this, many poetic passages glowed, like Alpine roses, among his massive sentences.

A poem by Rev. Dr. William Allen, of Northampton, ex-president of Bowdoin College, followed the sermon, and, if not such poetry as Bryant would have discoursed, it was excellent local history and topography, and well fitted to stimulate and gratify local pride. Dr. Allen was a scholar and biographical writer of decided merit; but his special claim to the position assigned him at the Jubilee was that he was a son of Rev. Thomas Allen, the first minister of Pittsfield and the "Fighting Parson of Bennington Field;" and that, succeeding his father in 1811, he had preached six years in the pulpit from which he read his poem; so that he might well have been regarded as a connecting link between the Berkshire men of the Revolution and those of the Jubilee time.

The oration on the second day, by Judge Joshua A. Spencer, was a terse *résumé* of Berkshire history, told with grace and spirit. Nature, grown more kindly, permitted it to be delivered, with other interesting exercises, from the platform on the hill. Up to this time this hill had been known simply as the "Childs Farm." But Rev. Dr. John Todd, the chairman of the Pittsfield committee, in his farewell address at the close of the Jubilee, in the dinner pavilion, said:

"We have been thinking how we could erect some monument of this Jubilee. In our wisdom we have spoken of several; but, after all, God has been before us; and his mighty hand hath reared the monument. That hill from which we came to this pavilion will hereafter bear the name of JUBILEE HILL; and when our heads are laid in the grave, and we have passed away, and are forgotten, we hope that our children and our children's children will walk over that beautiful spot, and say, 'Here our fathers celebrated the Berkshire Jubilee.' This monument shall stand as long as the footstool of God shall remain."

The great assemblage gave a ringing response to these words; and the name was fixed forever.

The Jubilee Dinner.

The successive parts of the Jubilee were remarkably well balanced; but the dinner was singularly memorable: the intellectual portion being an expansion of the thought and concentrated essence of the feeling which marked the preceding demonstration. Its story is certainly pertinent to our present essay, as Dr. Holmes was a conspicuous figure in it.

The main streets of Pittsfield that run north and south are, for some three-quarters of a mile, bordered by plains. Near the northern end of this distance there was in 1812 a large, perfectly level, open field. This attracted the attention of Maj.-Gen. H. A. S. Dearborn, who was organizing the Northern Military Department for the war that was just commencing; and he selected it as a site for a cantonment—a post of rendezvous, organization, and training for regiments raised in New England, and for the confinement of prisoners of war. Pittsfield had been chosen for the cantonment on account of its defensible position among the hills: a protection for which, at the Jubilee, years afterward, the assembled people returned thanks by singing with enthusiasm Mrs. Hemans' "Hymn of the Mountain Christians," of which we quote one verse:

DINNER-TABLES, PAVILION, Etc.
Berkshire Jubilee—1844. (From an old print.)

"For the strength of the hills, we bless thee,
 Our God, our fathers' God.
Thou hast made thy children mighty
 By the touch of the mountain sod.
Thou hast fixed our ark of refuge
 Where the spoiler's foot ne'er trod ;
For the strength of the hills we bless thee,
 Our God, our fathers' God."

Barracks were erected for the cantonment and occupied by many of the soldiers who won honor in the northern campaigns, and by more than two thousand of the prisoners captured by them; the privates among the latter seeming to enjoy their captivity better than campaigning.

When the war was over the barracks gave place to three large buildings erected for the Berkshire Gymnasium, a high school for young men, founded on a peculiar German model by Professor Chester Dewey, one of the foremost American men of science of his time, and one who did a great work as a pioneer in the study of Western Massachusetts geology, mineralogy, and natural history generally. Professor Dewey having discontinued the gymnasium, to accept a professorship in the Rochester University, the buildings were occupied in 1844 by the Pittsfield Young Ladies' Institute, which, although recently founded, had already attained a national standing. Before these buildings, a pavilion for the Jubilee dinner was erected, in which tables were spread for a thousand guests.

The president of the day was George N. Briggs, who was then serving the first of seven terms as Governor of the Commonwealth after six in Congress: an admirable selection, not solely because Governor Briggs was the most eminent citizen of the town and county in official rank; but because he was unsurpassed in qualifications to preside at a festal table like this: never-failing tact, self-possession, and knowledge of men, ready and never misplaced wit and humor, wonderful familiarity with Berkshire character, history, tradition, and anecdote, together with the happiest faculty for making use of his local lore.

Some thirty sons of Berkshire responded to the president's call for short speeches or "sentiments;" all of them men of note in their several homes, and some of wider fame. Among them, besides several who have been named in other connections, were President Heman Humphrey of Amherst College—who before and after that presidency was an intense and ardent Pittsfield man—Rev. Drs. Orville and Chester Dewey, Theodore Sedgwick, of New York and Stockbridge; John Mills, of Springfield, and Julius Rockwell, the successor of Governor Briggs in Congress. An interesting speaker was Rev. Joshua Noble Danforth, of Alexandria, Virginia, a son of Pittsfield's Revolutionary hero, Col. Joshua Danforth; who said: "We stand here to-day, forty in relationship—twenty-five of us the direct descendants of David Noble of Williamstown—the upright judge, the exemplary Christian."

A peculiarly pleasant and striking incident of the day was the speech and the reading of Leigh Hunt's poem, "Abou Ben Adhem," by William Charles Macready, the distinguished English tragedian; which, with Mrs. Kemble's grand Berkshire ode, made a contribution to the occasion from the British stage that was little to be expected.

Another pleasant and notable feature was the presence of Rev. Dr. David Dudley Field, of Stockbridge, the first historian of Berkshire County, with two of his famous sons, David Dudley and Cyrus W. Naturally the great lawyer was the spokesman of the family: but it is not for that we now specially recall him. In President Hopkins' sermon there occurred the following passage: "Probably most of us have read—for it was in an old New England school-book—of that 'Journey of a Day' that was a picture of human life. And, if it were given us to make the journey of a day that should be, not in its events, but in its scenery, the picture of our lives, where should we rather choose to make it than through the length of our Berkshire? What could be better than to watch the rising of the sun from the top of

Greylock, and his setting from the Eagle's Nest?"

"This passage so fastened itself on Mr. Field's mind" that he followed its suggestions, the very next week; and his spirited account of the experience the excursion brought him was widely published in the journals of the time under the title of "A Journey of a Day," and is reproduced in the recent superb edition of his writings. "The entire length of the county"— he wrote—"from north to south is fifty miles; and if the ascent of Greylock is made the evening before, so that the journey may begin at sunrise, it is possible in thirteen hours to pass down the valley, ascend the Dome of the Taconics, and get a last view of the setting sun from the Eagle's Nest." This he accomplished: passing through Williamstown, New Ashford, Lanesboro, Pittsfield, Lenox, Stockbridge, Great Barrington; and, over the Dome of the Taconics in Egremont, into the wild, awe-inspiring gorge of the far-famed Bash-Bish Falls in the western side of Mount Washington, where, among the other almost Alpine features, a vast wall of rock rises two hundred feet, beetling twenty-five feet beyond its base at its top; the Eagle's Nest, from which Mr. Field and his companion had a glorious view of the setting sun; Greylock, Williamstown, Lanesboro, Pittsfield, Lenox, Stockbridge, Great Barrington, the Dome, and the Eagle's Nest: what a carcanet of golden landscapes jeweled with precious memories these names call to mind! And to each and all the great jurist dealt poetic justice, both as to scenery and to story. We can, however, only quote his words regarding the Jubilee, and so much of those concerning Pittsfield as relate to the town as its seat.

Arriving at Pontoosuc Lake, which he locates in Lanesboro, although half its surface is in Pittsfield, Mr. Field writes:

"One feature of uncommon beauty, the place [Lanesboro'] has: its Pontoosuc Lake, or Shoonke Moonke, as it is sometimes called. It covers six hundred acres; and its bright waters, the road along its margin, and the tall trees that shade it make you sorry to leave it. We could not stay, but hurried on. to Pittsfield. What shall we say of Pittsfield; the hospitable, the beautiful? Just fresh from the Jubilee—fresh from the open houses and the open hearts of her people—we drove into the village, with the scenes of those two days fresh in our vision. The intervening week had vanished. We stood again on Jubilee Hill; we went down to the field where the feast was spread; we laughed under the Old Elm; we saw our friends—our fellows; as goodly a company as we shall see again for many a day. Truly it was a high festival: one worthy to be commemorated—to be repeated."

"The valley of the Housatonic here widens to its greatest breadth. Poontoosuck, the Indian name (pity it was not retained) signifies 'a field for the deer.' Pleasant place for hunting the Indians must have found it; and pleasant, too, for sojourn it is for the white man."

We must content us with one more contemporary description of the Jubilee; or a portion of one. It is from the pen of Catherine Sedgwick—there could be no better representatives of the people of southern Berkshire at the Jubilee, and of their feeling regarding it than Dudley Field and Catherine Sedgwick. An official report of the proceedings on the two days of the festival was published in an octavo volume, and Miss Sedgwick contributed to it a five-page *résumé* of the story, written in the Hebraic manner. We quote a few of the more detachable verses.

. . . .

"Hath not the Lord given us rest on every side! Now we will proclaim a Jubilee.—We will go up to our Jerusalem! We will worship in the temples of our fathers. We will kiss the sod that covers the graves of our kindred; and we will sit ourselves down in the old places where their shadows will pass before us!

"We will rejoice and make merry with our brethren; and Memory and Hope shall be our pleasant ministers. And we will lay our hearts together, and stir up the smouldering embers of old friendships till the fire burns within us: and this, even this sacred fire, will we transmit to our children's children.

"And even as they said, so did they; and in the summer solstice, with one heart and one mind, did they come together: the Pilgrims from afar and the Sojourners at home. Even from the valley of the Mississippi came they; and from the yet farther country of the Missouri, and from the Land of the Sun, even from the Southland; and from all the goodly lands about Massachusetts.

. . . .

"And they gathered together, a multitude of people, old men and elder women, young men and fair young maidens, and much children—a very great company were they.

"And a great heart was in the people of Pittsfield; and they opened the doors of their pleasant dwellings and bade their brethren enter therein. And they spread fine linen on their beds, and they covered their tables with the fat of the land; for the Lord had greatly blessed the people of Pittsfield.

"And they said to all their brethren: Come now and enter in and freely take of our abundance; for, lo, have we not spread our tables for you, and hath not the angel of sleep dressed our beds, that our brethren may sleep therein?

"And the faces of their brethren shone, and they entered in; and they said: It was a true report we heard of thee; thy land doth excel, and thou hast greatly increased the riches and the beauty thereof."

Such was the occasion on which Oliver Wendell Holmes first addressed a Berkshire audience; and such were the men and women associated with him in it.

Dr. Holmes' Speech and Poem.

Governor Briggs having made a cordial, interesting, and appropriate speech of welcome, to which Judge Betts responded in the same vein, the governor announced a poem by Dr. Holmes. The poet was already not unknown to fame, although very far from that which afterward celebrated his name; and its announcement was received with ringing cheers and cries of "Come forward!" The president suggested that he should rather follow the example of Judge Betts, and mount the table; remarking that this would be an advance on some old-fashioned feasts, where the tendency was rather to get under the table than upon it. Dr. Holmes followed this advice and took the table; and when the renewed cheers subsided read the following speech and poem.

He asked to be allowed, before he opened the paper in his hand, to assure his friends of the reason why he found himself there. He said:

"Inasmuch as the company express willingness to hear historical incidents, any little incident which shall connect me with those to whom I cannot claim to be a brother, seems to be fairly brought forward. One of my earliest recollections is of an annual pilgrimage made by my parents to the west. The young horse was brought up, fatted by a week's rest and high feeding, prancing and caracoling to the door. It came to the corner and was soon over the western hills. He was gone a fortnight; and one afternoon—it always seems to me it was a sunny afternoon—we saw an equipage crawling from the west toward the old homestead; the young horse, who set out fat and prancing, worn thin and reduced by a long journey—the chaise covered with dust, and all speaking of a terrible crusade, a formidable pilgrimage. Winter-evening stories told me where—to Berkshire, to the borders of New York, to the old domain, owned so long that there seemed a kind of hereditary love for it. Many years passed away, and I traveled down the beautiful Rhine. I wished to see the equally beautiful Hudson.

I found myself at Albany; a few hours' ride brought me to Pittsfield, and I went to the little spot, the scene of this pilgrimage—a mansion—and found it surrounded by a beautiful meadow, through which the winding river made its course in a thousand fantastic curves; the mountains reared their heads around it, the blue air which makes our city-pale cheeks again to deepen with the hue of health, coursing about it pure and free. I recognized it as the scene of the annual pilgrimage. Since then I have made an annual visit to it.

"In 1735, Hon. Jacob Wendell, my grandfather in the maternal line, bought a township not then laid out—the township of Poontoosuck—and that little spot which we still hold is the relic of twenty-four thousand acres of baronial territory. When I say this, no feeling which can be the subject of ridicule animates my bosom. I know too well that the hills and rocks outlast our families. I know we fall upon the places we claim, as the leaves of the forest fall, and as passed the soil from the hands of the original occupants into the hands of my immediate ancestors, I know it must pass from me and mine; and yet with pleasure and pride I feel I can take every inhabitant by the hand and say, If I am not a son or a grandson, or even a nephew of this fair county, I am at least allied to it by hereditary relation."

POEM OF WELCOME.

Come back to your Mother, ye children, for shame,
Who have wandered like truants, for riches or fame!
With a smile on her face and a sprig on her cap,
She calls you to feast from her bountiful lap.

Come out from your alleys, your courts and your lanes,
And breathe, like young eagles, the air of our plains:
Take a whiff from our fields, and your excellent wives
Will declare it's all nonsense insuring your lives.

Come you of the law, who can talk if you please
Till the man in the moon will allow it's a cheese,
And leave "the old lady, that never tells lies,"
To sleep with her handkerchief over her eyes.

Ye healers of men, for a moment decline
Your feats in the rhubarb and ipecac line;
While you shut up your turnpike, your neighbors can go
The old roundabout road to the regions below.

You clerk, on whose ears are a couple of pens,
And whose head is an ant-hill of units and tens;
Though Plato denies you, we welcome you still
As a featherless biped, in spite of your quill.

Poor drudge of the city, how happy he feels
With the burs on his legs and the grass at his heels;
No dodger behind, his bandanas to share,
No constable grumbling "You mustn't walk there."

In yonder green meadow, to memory dear,
He slaps a mosquito and brushes a tear;
The dew-drops hang round him on blossoms and shoots,
He breathes but one sigh for his youth and his boots.

There stands the old school-house, hard by the old
   church;
That tree at its side had the flavor of birch;
Oh sweet were the days of his juvenile tricks,
Though the prairie of youth had so many "big licks."

By the side of yon river he weeps and he slumps,
His boots filled with water as if they were pumps;
Till, sated with rapture, he steals to his bed,
With a glow in his heart and a cold in his head.

'Tis past—he is dreaming—I see him again;
His ledger returns as by legerdemain;
His neck-cloth is damp, with an easterly flaw,
And he holds in his fingers an omnibus straw.

He dreams the shrill gust is a blossomy gale,
That the straw is a rose from his dear native vale;
And murmurs, unconscious of space and of time,
"A 1, Extra-super—Oh, isn't it Prime!"

Oh, what are the prizes we perish to win,
To the first little "shiner" we caught with a pin!
No soil upon earth is as dear to our eyes
As the soil we first stirred in terrestrial pies!

Then come from all parties, and parts, to our feast,
Though not at the "Astor," we'll give you at least
A bite at an apple, a seat on the grass,
And the best of cold—water—at nothing a glass.

II.

THE WENDELL FAMILY.

Jacob Wendell in Boston—Connection with Old Boston Families—Buys Township now Pittsfield—His Descendants—Holmes' Genealogy—Phillips' Genealogy—Wendell Phillips—Oliver Wendell in Pittsfield —Curious Incidents—Oliver Wendell Fierce for Moderation—Friendship with the Van Schaacks.

DR. HOLMES' reference in his Jubilee speech to his great-grandfather's, Col. Jacob Wendell's, early property in the township of Poontoosuck was all that the occasion demanded; or at least all that the brevity in speeches enjoined by the president permitted; as, with his usual courtesy for those who were to follow him, he declined to avail himself of the evident general desire of his listeners to waive the rule of limitation in his behalf. Still something more in detail and more precise than family tradition will have interest for many readers.

Jacob Wendell was born at Albany, in 1691, of good old Holland lineage. About the year 1720 he removed to Boston, where he prospered, becoming a wealthy merchant, an influential citizen, a member of the Provincial Council, and, besides other important civil offices, colonel of the local militia regiment. He held this command in 1744, when Boston greatly dreaded invasion by a French naval armament, and was one of seven magnates who demanded a town meeting to "consider steps for the better protection of the town and its approaches." The steps were taken, and in 1745, when Governor Shirley, returning in triumph after the capture of Louisburgh, landed at "the castle" from the frigate "Massachusetts," he was met by Colonel Wendell's regiment and Colonel Pollard's Cadets, and escorted into town amid the unbounded enthusiastic demonstrations of the people; the day being "given up to jollification." Afterward Colonel Wendell was commander of the " Ancient and Honorable Artillery Company." His residence in Boston was a brick mansion, notable for its time, on the corner of Tremont and School streets, opposite to that on which King's Chapel was built in 1749.

Soon after Colonel Wendell began business in Boston there sprang up something very like a western fever for speculation in the unappropriated lands in the county of Hampshire, which then included the present Hampshire, Berkshire, Hampden, and Franklin. In 1735 the General Court granted three townships of these lands, each six miles square, to the town of

Boston, in consideration for its heavy expenditures for free schools and the support of its poor; and also because it paid one-fifth of the entire annual tax of the Province.

Certain not very light conditions were attached to this grant, and three members of the Council and four of the House were appointed a commission to see that they were faithfully complied with. Colonel Wendell was one of the commissioners, and in 1736 he bought at auction the inchoate right to one of these townships, which, when selected and the title to it duly confirmed, was Poontoosuck. It the nappeared that Colonel Wendell had bought as well for his kinsman, Edward Livingston, of Albany, as for himself. It was also found that Col. John Stoddard, of Northampton, had a prior grant of 1,000 acres of the best uplands, and had also purchased the Indian title to a tract in which the whole township was included. Circumstances had made Colonels Wendell and Stoddard thoroughly and personally familiar with the whole region to which their choice was confined,* and all the grantees knew well all that in forest days could be known of the region which lay in and around the spot which is now

---

*The Upper and Lower Housatonic townships, embracing what are now the towns of Sheffield and Great Barrington and the township now Stockbridge and West Stockbridge, had already been appropriated.

Pittsfield, as it has been described to the reader. And they were so well satisfied with it that, wise men as they were, they preferred, rather than to make a new selection, to compromise upon a joint and equal undivided ownership.

The French and Indian wars defeated for years their repeated earnest efforts to effect a settlement of the township, and none was made until 1752. But, in accordance with the terms of the grant, sixty-three one-hundred-acre settling lots were in 1738 laid out in a central portion of the township, in a compact form. These were in due time disposed of in one way or another.

The remainder of the 24,040 acres, which was the exact measurement of the grant, was held in common until January, 1760; a division in 1752 having, in 1754, on an appeal by Colonel Wendell, been set aside by a competent court as improperly made. The abrogated division was made on a petition from Capt. Charles Goodrich, to whom Colonel Wendell had sold an undivided third part of his interest in the "commons." Livingston, in 1743, sold his entire interest to a syndicate of prominent western Massachusetts citizens for £3,000. Colonel Stoddard died in 1748, leaving his Poontoosuck lands to his widow and his sons, Israel and Solomon, all afterward residents of note in Pittsfield. Such was the ownership of the "commons" lands when in January, 1760, a competent and scrupulously impartial commission, appointed by the court with the approval of all concerned, rendered a satisfactory report apportioning them to the proprietors in severalty. It divided the lands into squares, averaging about three hundred acres in size; and carefully classed them as first, second, and third rate in quality. These squares were distributed among the owners to whom they were respectively assigned, not contiguously, but intermixed all over the township. Colonel Wendell received twenty-two, and chance seems to have favored him in the natural beauty of some of them. All of the north and west shores of Lake Onota fell to him, and also Square No. 5, afterward the farm of the Revolutionary hero, Israel Dickinson; and later the park-like estate attached to the summer residence of Judge Benjamin R. Curtis. Its next owner, Hon. Ensign H. Kellogg, gave it the name of Morningside, which is now familiar as that of a busy and populous section of the city. The acquisition that Colonel Wendell most prized, and which is also of most interest to us in the present connection, was that comprised in Squares 56 and 57, which included the Canoe Meadows. In a plot of the township which must have been a Wendell family paper, there is written across the location of these squares this minute: "Colonel Wendell's meadow included in these two lots; chiefly valuable."

The old Wendells appreciated this feature, as Dr. Holmes did when he built his summer villa on Square 56, to overlook the meadows and the Housatonic flowing through them.

Both Colonel Stoddard and Colonel Wendell plainly looked upon their Poontoosuck purchase in a different light from that in which they viewed other places in which they owned lands. "The Great New Englander" died before settlement there was practicable; but it was in accordance with his wish that his widow and sons made it their home. In some early archives the inchoate town is styled Wendellstown, and Colonel Wendell manifested his kindly feeling toward it in many ways, as many of his descendants have done; among them Dr. Holmes and Wendell Phillips—whose lines of descent we will trace in outline.

Some of Colonel Wendell's Descendants.

Jacob Wendell was born, in 1691, at Albany. His father, John Wendell, died while he was an infant, and in 1695 his widowed mother married Capt. John Schuyler. Her maiden name was Elizabeth Staats, and Jacob was named for her brother, Jacob Staats, who was one of the sponsors at his christening in the old Dutch church. Not long after his removal to Boston, he married Sarah, daughter of Dr. James Oliver, "a famous physician who graduated at Harvard in 1680 and died in 1703." Several descendants of this marriage have made their mark in the political, literary, and legal history of Massachusetts; prominently among them Judge Oliver Wendell, Oliver Wendell Holmes and his son, the present Judge Oliver Wendell Holmes; John Phillips, the first Mayor of Boston, and his son Wendell Phillips.

It would bewilder any but the best-trained genealogist even to attempt arranging the web of direct and collateral relationships with the Hutchinsons, the Olivers, the Brattles, and other provincial Boston gentry into which Colonel Wendell's marriage introduced Dr. Holmes' ancestry; to say nothing about interweaving it with the Schuylers, Livingstons, and others of like degree in old Dutch rank, with whom Historian Henry C. Van Schaack affiliates the Wendells. It has been said that the poet was very proud of his descent, and that this pride colored both his life and many of his literary productions. It may have manifested itself in his Berkshire, as in his Boston, social life: but we scrupulously avoid obtruding upon either. In his relations to the Berkshire public and in his Berkshire poems, there is, however, nothing in the slightest degree to indicate ancestral pride, except the *noblesse oblige* which governed him everywhere and always; unless his natural and necessary allusions to Colonel Wendell in his Jubilee address and in some letters may be counted as such an indication. We will therefore only state, and that briefly, the lines of descent from Colonel Wendell, of Dr. Holmes and Wendell Phillips; adding the latter because the two cousins expressed a like interest in Pittsfield on account of their common ancestor's relations to it; and also because, wide apart as the political agitations of the country during their middle life drifted them, they always had a true, kindly, cousinly pride in each other's genius and fame.*

The Holmes Genealogy.—The youngest child of Jacob and Sarah [Oliver] Wendell was Oliver Wendell, who was born in 1734. He married Mary, daughter of Edward Jackson. Their daughter, Sarah, married Rev. Abiel Holmes, of Cambridge, a theological and historical

---

* We believe this to be true of Dr. Holmes; and we know it to be so of Mr. Phillips, as frequent conversations with him concerning the genealogy and history of the Wendell family gave us opportunity to learn. Mr. Phillips had a decided natural love for historical and genealogical studies, and had not duty called him to another field might have become the great historian of Massachusetts who is still to come. He once, with evident feeling, showed the present writer a handsome volume, compiled, if memory serves us correctly, by himself; which gave an account of those of his ancestors who are buried in the King's Chapel burial-ground.

writer of note; and became the mother of Oliver Wendell Holmes.

The Phillips Genealogy.—Margaret, one of Colonel Wendell's daughters, married William Phillips, a member of an old and distinguished family and himself lieutenant-governor of Massachusetts. Their son, John, who, in 1822, was elected the first mayor of Boston, married Sarah Whalley, and became the father of Wendell Phillips.

After Colonel Wendell's death his lands in Pittsfield were divided among his heirs, and the squares assigned to each respectively are designated, on the chart before mentioned, by initials. Square 56, on which Dr. Holmes built his villa, fell to Oliver Wendell and his brother, John Mico, who also received several other squares; some jointly, some severally. John Mico Wendell married Catherine Brattle, a descendant of Thomas Brattle, the founder of the distinguished Boston family of that name; and some of his Pittsfield land, in one way or another, passed into the hands of one of its cadets, who settled upon it; thus planting a branch of it in the town, where it still has representatives. Both the wife and mother of John Mico Wendell were descendants of Governors Dudley and Bradstreet. In 1791, Oliver Wendell, Catherine Wendell, Margaret Phillips (grandmother of Wendell Phillips) and other heirs of the first owner of the township, still retained 1,200 of its 24,000 acres and were taxed £4 toward the building in that year of the town's second meeting-house: the same in which, fifty-eight years afterward, Dr. Holmes read his famous cattle-show poem, "The Ploughman."

Oliver Wendell was, as a summer resident and owner of real estate in Pittsfield, more closely identified with its general affairs than any other member of the Wendell family; Dr. Holmes' relations to it being, except in the ownership of his country-seat, purely of a literary character. As to Oliver Wendell's life in his ordinary home: Born at Boston in 1734, and graduating from Harvard at the age of nineteen, he followed in the footsteps of his father as a merchant; and in 1783 was one of the founders and directors of the Massachusetts Bank, the first institution of the kind in New England. He was representative from Boston in 1771–72; selectman in 1733–34; and a delegate to the Provincial Congresses of 1775 and 1776, some of the other members of the delegation being John Hancock, Samuel Adams, and Gen. Joseph Warren. After the Revolution he was for several years one of the Executive Council of the Commonwealth, and for many judge of probate for Suffolk County, and a trustee of Harvard College.

During the Revolution, and in preparation

for it, he was prominent as an active and influential Whig: so much so that local tradition has it that early in the great struggle he came to Pittsfield, and made arrangements with the occupant of his farm on Square 56, in accordance with which the lease was to be vacated and Mr. Wendell take possession of the place with all its appurtenances, including the furniture, in case the turn of affairs at Boston should drive him to the refuge of the hills; and that this was the origin of the family custom of annually visiting Pittsfield. We apprehend that in this instance, as in most others, tradition is truth a little scratched. The facts are probably these: While Boston was occupied by British troops residence there was impossible for a Whig of Oliver Wendell's standing. Colonel Wendell had initiated the custom alluded to, and it probably suggested to his son the convenience of Pittsfield as a place of temporary residence, when his presence was not needed near the center of Revolutionary operations, or of refuge if any temporary reverse should befall the patriots. But the annual pilgrimage was not yet so invariable as it afterward became, and the details of preparation for it at the farm were not so complete. What Mr. Wendell did was, we fancy, to make arrangements to remedy this. In the earliest years of the Revolution and those immediately preceding it, the Tory element in

Pittsfield was suppressed with a strong hand; but it had been powerful, and was still far from being annihilated. Its leaders were secretly in conference with the British generals, and, if the Royal Government of the Province had been fully and permanently restored, Pittsfield would have been no more safe as a refuge from its vengeance than Boston itself, however it might have been with some of the neighboring mountain towns, with their rugged recesses.

This much at least is certain, that Judge Wendell did firmly establish and make definite arrangements for the custom of keeping a resident farmer upon the place and making an annual pilgrimage to it; and that he did himself adhere to it very rigidly. And therewith is connected a tradition quaint enough to have pleased a humorist like the author of the wonderful "One-Hoss Shay." Gentlemen of his class and time knew how to criticise the luxuries of the table and the proprieties of cookery quite as well at least as the most accomplished diner-out now does. A modern reader new to mildewed manuscripts would often be surprised to come across, in their letters and diaries, glowing descriptions of dinners technically accurate even to the elaborate *menu du repas;* and he might be still more astonished to read their praises of rare and luxurious viands well served at taverns far inland, as, for instance, in Vermont. Nevertheless Judge Wendell, in some of his earlier rides from Boston to Berkshire, had so disagreeable experience of country tavern dinners that it demanded a remedy; and he devised one. His favorite dish, when the variety afforded by his own table was not to be had, was roast or broiled chicken; but he saw that his order for it at his wayside inn was invariably instantly followed by a mad rush for the barnyard, where, after a breathless chase, an unhappy fowl was hunted down, slaughtered, perhaps before his eyes, and served up to him before the life was well out of its body. Disgusted by this barbarism, he ever afterward, before he left home to cross the mountains, had a dressed fowl placed in his carriage to be cooked and eaten at the tavern where he first dined; and where he was supplied with another prepared in the same way, to undergo a like seasoning for the next day's repast; and so on for the three, four, or more days of his journey.

A lady, now long since passed away, used to speak of the carriage in which Judge Wendell made these journeys and rode about town as a marvel of magnificence in her childhood's eyes and in those of her young companions, who went out to meet its coming as those of later days do that of a circus. But the only one of its splendors that she could distinctly recall was the green blinds, which it seems answered for curtains.

Decided as Judge Wendell's political principles were, and ardent as was his Revolutionary zeal, he was yet so noted for liberality to those who differed from him in sentiment and action that his compatriots pronounced him "fierce for moderation." Some instances illustrative of this trait in his character have a local Pittsfield flavor. In 1777 Peter and Henry Van Schaack, citizens of much distinction in Albany and Kinderhook, refusing to take the oath of allegiance to the government newly established in New York after the Declaration of Independence, were "exiled:" that is, placed under surveillance in places assigned them for residence in other States; in some of which they suffered pretty rough usage in the way of close confinement and otherwise. Boston and Pittsfield, however, were not among these inhospitable involuntary homes, notwithstanding the intense radicalism of the Pittsfield Whigs. Henry Van Schaack, being permitted to choose a residence in one of several Berkshire towns, after brief trials of Stockbridge and Richmond, selected Pittsfield. In Berkshire he suffered little persecution for opinion's sake, being perhaps protected by the personal friendship of Theodore Sedgwick, who was as "fierce for moderation" as Oliver Wendell, who appears to have intermitted his visits to Pittsfield in some of the latter years of the Revolution. At any rate, Mr. Van Schaack, a man of property and of much intellectual ability, had so pleasant experience of the place of his captivity that he bought the confiscated estate of a brother loyalist who had fled to England, and, after the peace, built upon it the spacious and substantial mansion now known as Broadhall, and lived in it many years, an active, public-spirited, and influential citizen of the town, and a devoted trustee of Williams College.

Peter Van Schaack's son, Henry C. Van Schaack, of Manlius, N. Y., published a memoir of his father and left in manuscript one of his uncle and namesake; from which we condense his statements of their relations with Judge Wendell.

When Peter Van Schaack went to Boston, an exile, in February, 1777, "he experienced very liberal and gentlemanly treatment from Oliver Wendell, one of the leading patriots of the Massachusetts Bay. This gentleman evidently discovered that, in the person of the exile, no common character had been sent to the selectmen of Boston; while the latter was deeply impressed by the consideration and humanity exhibited toward him, a perfect stranger to the place, its inhabitants, and public authorities, and with naught to recommend him but his frank and elevated gentlemanly appearance and conversation, during a few days' stay in town.

The acquaintance formed under so forbidding circumstances led to a long and interesting correspondence, some portion of which has been published. . . ." After Henry Van Schaack became a citizen of Massachusetts, he visited Boston, and "made a point of calling upon Judge Wendell with no other introduction than his personal representation that he came to return his thanks for Mr. Wendell's conduct toward his brother, when he was exiled to Boston in 1777. This call resulted in an acquaintance that immediately ripened into a close and lasting friendship; during which they kept up an intimate correspondence."

It might be suspected that the intimate friendship of Messrs. Wendell and Van Schaack was, at least in part, due to the fact that, in the bitter political strife which resulted in the adoption of the Federal Constitution, and the organization of the Federal and Democratic parties, both were Federalists of the most extreme type, and never ceased to be so. But another incident showed him equally kind and courteous to his Democratic opponents. Rev. Thomas Allen, the first Pittsfield minister, was very far from being "fierce for moderation" in his Jeffersonian Democracy. His son of the same name, a young man of the highest promise for political eminence, was equally devoted to the same principles, although manifestation of his feeling was doubtless modified by a more intimate acquaintance with the world beyond the mountains. He was the idol of the Democratic party in Pittsfield; but he died in Boston while representing the town in the Legislature of 1806, and was buried in the King's Chapel tomb of the Federal Wendells. Remembering what the town of Pittsfield was to the Wendell family, such a burial would seem not at all remarkable, but rather a matter-of-course, had personal feeling between political opponents been as it is to-day; but in the early part of the century personal antipathies were so interwoven with political antagonisms that this must be counted another evidence of Judge Wendell's exceptional kindly courtesy.

Nevertheless, nothing hindered his hearty maintenance of his Federalism in his country home, where he was inspiring and helpful to his fellows in politics. At that time political feeling in Pittsfield disturbed church and parochial harmony to such an extent that the Federal church members and parishioners were driven to organize a separate church and separate parish; and finally to erect a meetinghouse. In all this, they had the warm sympathy of the Boston Federalists; but none of them appear to have contributed pecuniary aid except Judge Wendell, who gave liberally toward the building of the meeting-house and the support in it of public worship, which he attended regularly when he was in town. In 1817 the two churches and parishes were reunited as the First Congregational; and among the church plate there is still a solid silver christening-bowl that was presented by him to the Union Church. His voluntary contribution for the building of the Union meeting-house was much larger than the tax that was assessed upon him and other Wendell heirs for the building of that erected in 1791. It is a curious instance of the incidental connection of minor and widely separated events, that in 1849 Dr. Holmes saw the accidental burning of the long-disused Union meeting-house, and that it probably suggested to him these fine lines in " The Astrea," written in 1850.

"The oriole drifting like a flake of fire,
Torn by a whirlwind from a blazing spire."

O. W. HOLMES'S VILLA

In 1849.

III.

DR. HOLMES' SUMMER VILLA AND LIFE IN IT.

The Villa—Letters to a Pittsfield Lady and Her Reminiscences—Letter to a School-Teacher—Blackberries and other Berries—The Canoe Meadows—The Holmes Pine.

IN the summer of 1848, four years after the Jubilee, Dr. Holmes built a pretty villa, crowning a knoll on his inherited estate: a plain, neat structure well adapted to his purposes. In his journal of August 5, 1848, Longfellow wrote: " Drove over, in the afternoon, to Dr. Holmes' house on the old Wendell farm—a snug little place, with views of the river and the mountains." This is tersely truthful. The river and the mountains gave the house its charm for its owner, who never tired of their praises. Every reader of " The Autocrat" will remember his fondness also for trees and his dissertation upon the specific merits of those distinguished for merit. We suspect that his friend, Dr. Orville Dewey, enjoyed his eulogy upon the Sheffield Elm, which he described as "equally remarkable for size and for perfection of form." He had "seen nothing in Berkshire County that came near it, and few to compare with it anywhere." His irreverent remark that "the poor old Pittsfield Elm lived on its past reputation," and that "a wig of false leaves was indispensable to make it presentable," might be less palatable to the lovers of that venerable—and now fallen—tree, did they fail to consider that it was written, not unkindly, but in the same spirit that dictated the poem of "The Last Leaf."

But, well as Dr. Holmes loved trees, his Holmes Road farm, when he determined to build a summer home upon it, was almost entirely destitute of them. Thanks to him, as we shall see, it is now very far from that. But, in telling of this home and Dr. Holmes' life in it, we must call in valuable aid. It is our general design to avoid all mention of Dr. Holmes' private life in Pittsfield; as one not personally familiar with it would be likely to commit blunders, and probable injustice. Remembering, however, a Pittsfield lady who, like her distinguished husband, was long an intimate friend of Dr. Holmes, and his frequent correspondent down to his latest years, the impulse was irresistible to fill what would otherwise have been "an aching void," by soliciting some reminiscences of the poet and such extracts from his letters as would serve to illustrate his local verse, the life he enjoyed while writing it, and his feeling toward the town. What follows is due to her kindly acquiescence.

REMINISCENT.

"Dr. Holmes' life in Pittsfield was fascinating to him, and to those who knew him here. Passing parts of fifteen years in Boston, we knew him and his family there, visiting them in both their Montgomery Place and Charles Street residences. When they came to make their summer home on Holmes Road we often exchanged visits. We frequently drove over at twilight, when the poet was at his best, and would show us, from his library windows, animals and birds in the outlines of the eastern hills; or, what pleased him most, 'General Taylor mounted on his horse.' When the shadows deepened, so that he could no longer see these phantasms, which even daylight did not reveal to us, he would say: 'Now, come into the dining-room, and we will have some caviare to the general.'

"He was not a 'society man'—observe what a wide difference in significance there is between 'society' and 'social,' when they are used as adjectives. Once, by much persuasion, he was induced to attend the first evening party that was given by a lady nearly connected by marriage with the poet Longfellow's wife; but he was ill at ease; and during the evening I said to him: 'Why, you are just like a boy!' The reply was ready: 'I like that!' he exclaimed, 'the best compliment of my life!'"

EXTRACTS FROM DR HOLMES' LETTERS.

February, 1856.—I have many nibbles for my place in Pittsfield, from Boston and New York; but it takes many nibbles to make a bite.

January 15, 1857.—Seven sweet summers, the happiest of my life. I wouldn't exchange the recollection of them for a suburban villa. One thing I shall always be glad of; that I planted seven hundred trees for somebody to sit in the shade of.

July 22, 1865.—I like to see worthless rich people succumb to the deserving poor who, beginning with sixpence or nothing, come out at last on Beacon Street, and have the sun in their windows all the year round. [A bit of sarcasm in this?—ED.]

July 16, 1872.—I am a pretty well-seasoned old stick of timber or you would have brought me to your purpose [to obtain a poem from him at the dedication of the soldiers' monument in the Pittsfield Park, when George William Curtis delivered the oration]. I have glorified your ploughman and tried to sanctify your cemetery. But I am older now—set in my ways. I want to put away all such things, lay up my heels and read story-books.—No! my dear madame; you cannot coax me—but it grieves me to say "No," to you.

December 8, 1885.—When you meet any one who, you think, remembers me, say that I am still loyal to the old place, . . . and that the very stones of it are as dear to me as were those of Jerusalem to the ancient Hebrews.

January 1, 1885.—A Happy New Year! And as many such as you can count, until you reach a hundred; and then begin again, if you like this planet well enough. . . . I delight in recalling the old scenes. Changed they must be; yet I seem to be carried back to the broad [East. —ED.] street, our usual drive on our way from the "Four Corners" and "Canoe Meadows" [The Wendell Farm], as my mother told me they called it. It seems too bad to take away the town's charming characteristics; but such a healthful, beautiful, central situation could not resist its destiny; and you must have a mayor, aldermen, and common council. But Greylock will remain, and you cannot turn the course of the Housatonic. I cannot believe that it is thirty years since I said "Good-bye," expecting to return the next season. As we passed the gate under the maple which may stand there now, we turned and looked at the house and at the Great Pine which stood—and I hope still stands—in its solitary grandeur and beauty; passed the two bridges to the railroad station— and, Good-bye, Dear Old Folks!

February 7, 1891.—I do so love to hear about dear old Pittsfield: what is done there and who does it; how the new city gets on; and all the rest.

March 12, 1891.—You are to be a city. Think of my little boy a Judge and able to send me to jail if I do not behave myself. I have given up my professorship, and am now in my literary shirt-sleeves.

October 12, 1893.—What a grand spunky town, Pittsfield is! You are to have "The Ancient and Honorable there;" of which my great-grandfather, Jacob Wendell, was colonel,— Great changes; but Greylock, the Housatonic and Pontoosuc still exist.

December 14, 1893.—Dear old Pittsfield! shall I ever have spunk enough to take another look at it? It would be both a pleasure and a poignant ache. The old outlines are there. The trees I planted would look kindly down upon me. But, alas! how much would be missing! And then, you are getting so grand and New Yorky, I should be lost in its splendor and wealth.

July 24, 1894.—It tires me to write now. I cannot give your letters to my secretary. My

THE GREAT PINE AT HOLMES' VILLA.
Pittsfield, Mass.

eyes are dim—my fingers crampy.—Were I forty years old, instead of three-score and twenty-four, I would try to buy my old place, *just as it was*, and be once more your summer neighbor. My habits are fixed. I am ill. Write and aid my convalescence with a lively manifesto from our blessed city of Pittsfield. The pendulum has a very short range of oscillation.

"Alas! it soon forever ceased to vibrate," adds his favored correspondent.

LETTER TO A SCHOOL-TEACHER.

We will quote one more characteristic letter of Dr. Holmes, which is cumulative as regards much in those already given; but which is also evidence of the great author's kindly regard for the little people who are to be the future readers of all authors, and his appreciation of those who are preparing them to be intelligent ones. It was written to Miss Fannie E. Brewster, a teacher in one of the Pittsfield grammar schools, who, in preparing her class for a rhetorical exercise upon the life and works of Dr. Holmes, asked him for a few words, to give them a keener interest in it. He replied promptly and pleasantly in a letter that will interest school-teachers and all who love children,—as who that has a heart does not?—as follows:

BOSTON, May 22, 1884.

MY DEAR MISS BREWSTER:

I drop all the papers in my hand, to write those few words you ask me for. The memory of Pittsfield is dear to me. How can I forget the seven blissful summers passed there? Most of my old Pittsfield friends are gone; but, if the younger generation still recall my name, I feel as if I had yet a home among you. Give my warm regards and best wishes to my young friends; and believe me,

Very truly yours,
OLIVER WENDELL HOLMES.

There are passages in some of Dr. Holmes' prose writings which show how observant he was of features in the region about his villa, that challenge observation less boldly than the mountains, the rivers, and the meadows; and they show how suggestive of thought even little things were to him. In one of his books he says:

"In Pittsfield I missed the huckleberry, the bayberry, the sweet fern, and the barberry. At least there were none near my residence, so far as I know. But we have blackberries—a great number of the high-bush kind. I wonder if others have observed what an imitative fruit it is. I have tasted the strawberry, the pineapple, and I do not know how many other flavors in it.

If you think a little and have read Darwin and Huxley, perhaps you will believe that it and all the fruits it tastes of may have come from a common progenitor."

For Dr. Holmes the blackberry seems to have been among berries what the mocking-bird is among birds. It would not be strange if the reader, the next time he enjoys a plate of blackberries—or better, when he eats them fresh from the bush—should be enabled by this paragraph to detect some of these borrowed flavors.

The sweet fern grows in abundance along the base of the Taconic hills some four or five miles west of Dr. Holmes' residence, and some of their summits are prolific of blueberries. To be sure the blueberry imperfectly supplies the place of the luscious black huckleberry; but then the huckleberry bush is often underlaid by a rattlesnake or two, while Pittsfield is as free as Ireland itself from that terror of rocky and swampy lands. A few bushes of the barberry grow sporadically on the hills, but they do not take kindly, or unkindly, to the soil, and cover acres of it with their prickly, although prettily adorned and spicily fruited, brambles, as they do in eastern Massachusetts and New Hampshire.

Here is another instance of Dr. Holmes' thoughtful observation of little things about his residence: The Canoe Meadows on his estate, so often mentioned in our story,—and on which he looked with pride from his library windows and the pleasant rear piazza of his villa—were so named because the Stockbridge Indians were accustomed to leave their birch canoes in them while they visited the graves of their fathers near the opposite shore of the Housatonic, which flows through them; and probably also while hunting or trapping in the neighborhood. This is his statement of and comment on his aboriginal findings there:

"At Cantabridge near the sea, I have once or twice turned up an Indian arrowhead in a fresh furrow. At Canoe Meadows in the Berkshire mountains, I have found Indian arrowheads. So everywhere, Indian arrowheads. Whether a hundred or a thousand years old, who knows? and who cares? There is no history to the red race. . . . A few instincts walking about on legs, and holding a tomahawk:—There is the Indian for all time."

There is an underlying touch of pathos in Dr. Holmes' mention of the great pine upon which his last look lingered when for the last time he left his home by the Housatonic. It was the only large and handsome tree on his estate when he inherited it, and we seem to remember a statement regarding it, from his own pen, more extended than that quoted. But, like many similar memories, it may be only seeming. At least, we cannot, for the life of us, recall when, and in what work, we read it, if we read it at all; and the seeming may have come from conversation or a dream. We can and do, however, present a fine portrait of the noble tree, from which a fair conception of it, as it now stands, may be gained.

IV.

A VISION OF THE HOUSATONIC RIVER.

Dr. Holmes Loved the River—Remembered It by the English River Cam—Loved also by Many Men and Women of Letters—The Poem.

Dr. Holmes' affection for the Housatonic River, and his pride in its graceful winding through his ancestral acres, within sight from his library windows, were manifested on every fitting opportunity. Probably as a humorist and proprietor of the Canoe Meadows, and perhaps as a "medicine man" as well, he approved the time-honored local pun that the best of all tonics is the Housatonic. A striking instance of his fond memory of the familiar stream appears in his "Hundred Days Trip to Europe" in 1886. During his visit to England he received the honorary degree of LL. D. from the University of Cambridge, there being some very flattering demonstrations of approval by the assembly while the ceremony of conferring it was going on. He gives a modest account of it in his book, and a pleasing one of the old college town. But even on an occasion when a good degree of personal pride would have been pardonable, he did not forget his old home, and his closing paragraph of the story is this:

"The University left a very deep impression on my mind, in which a few grand objects predominate over all the rest; all being delightful. I was fortunate enough to see the gathering of the boats, which is the last scene in the annual procession. The show was altogether lovely. The pretty river [the Cam] about as wide as the Housatonic, I should judge, as that slender stream flows through Canoe Meadow—my old Pittsfield residence—the gaily dressed people who crowded the banks, the boats with the gallant young oarsmen who handled them so skillfully made a picture not often excelled."

Dr. Holmes was not alone in his appreciation of

"The gentle river winding free
Through realms of peace and liberty."

Long ago, when the Housatonic wound its sinuous way through an almost unbroken and not altogether peaceful forest, the great student of man's will, Jonathan Edwards, recognized its beauty, and, doubtless, resting now and then from herculean labors in his liliputian mental workshop at Stockbridge, strolled across the street to enjoy it, and be soothed by the "warbling tone" of its rippling waters. Since that great thinker bade it adieu, other great thinkers of thoughts far other than his, but loving it as he did, have celebrated it in prose and verse until now it is well-nigh the most classic of American streams. Among those who have contributed to its fame, most of them having either permanent or temporary homes near its banks, are Catherine Sedgwick, William Cullen Bryant, David Dudley Field, Herman Melville, Henry Ward Beecher, Nathaniel Hawthorne, Fanny Kemble, Lydia Huntley Sigourney, Henry W. Longfellow, and Dr. William Allen, besides scores of minor writers. Its most marked tribute from Dr. Holmes' pen is " THE VISION OF THE HOUSATONIC RIVER," which was written and used as an epilogue to its author's lecture on Wordsworth. The reader will bear in mind its original purpose; and also that the book referred to in the eighth verse is Wordsworth's poems, with their introduction of English scenery, meadow-flora, and bird-life. In lieu of the lecture, we will preface the "Vision" with what the Autocrat wrote of the Housatonic and its surroundings in very poetic prose. After dwelling awhile on pleasant memories of a favorite Connecticut resort, the Autocrat continues:

"And again, once more among those other hills that shut in the amber-flowing Housatonic, —dark stream, but clear, like lucid orbs that shine between the lids of auburn-haired, sherry-wine-eyed demi-blondes,—in the home overlooking the winding stream and the smooth flat meadow; looked down upon by wild hills, where the tracks of bears and catamounts may yet sometimes be seen on the winter snow; facing the twin summits which rise, far north— the highest waves of the great land-storm in all this billowy region—suggestive to mad fancies of the breasts of a half-buried Titaness, stretched out by a stray thunderbolt and hastily hidden away beneath the leaves of the forest: in that home where seven blessed summers were passed, which stand in memory like the Seven Golden Candlesticks in the beatific vision of the holy dreamer . . . this long articulated sigh of reminiscences—this calenture which shows me the maple-shaded plains of Berkshire and the mountain-circled green of Grafton."

THE VISION.

Come, spread your wings as I spread mine
    And leave the crowded hall,
For where the eyes of twilight shine
    O'er evening's western wall.

These are the pleasant Berkshire hills,
    Each with its leafy crown;
Hark! from their sides a thousand rills
    Come singing sweetly down.

A thousand rills; they leap and shine,
    Strained through the mossy nooks,

Till, clasped in many a gathering twine,
    They swell a hundred brooks.

A hundred brooks, and still they run
    With ripple, shade, and gleam,
Till clustering all their braids in one,
    They flow a single stream.

A bracelet, spun from mountain mist,
    A silvery sash unwound,
With ox-bow curve and sinuous twist,
    It writhes to reach the "Sound."

This is my bark; a pigmy's ship;
    Beneath a child it rolls;
Fear not; one body makes it dip,
    But not a thousand souls.

Float we the grassy banks between;
    Without an oar we glide;
The meadows, sheets of living green,
    Unroll on either side.

Come, take the book we love so well,
    And let us read and dream.
We see whate'er its pages tell
    And sail an English stream.

Up to the clouds the lark has sprung,
    Still trilling as he flies;
The linnet sings as there he sung;
    The unseen cuckoo cries;

And daisies strew the banks along,
    And yellow kingcups shine,
With cowslips and a primrose throng,
    And humble celandine.

Ah, foolish dream! When Nature nursed
    Her daughter in the West,
Europe had drained one fountain first;
    She bared her other breast.

On the young planet's orient shore
    Her morning hand she tried;
Then turned the broad medallion o'er
    And stamped the sunset side.

Take what she gives; her pine's tall stem,
    Her elm with drooping spray;
She wears her mountain diadem
    Still in her own proud way.

Look on the forest's ancient kings,
    The hemlock's towering pride;
Yon trunk had twice a hundred rings
    And fell before it died.

Nor think that Nature saves her bloom
    And slights her new domain;
For us she wears her court costume;
    Look on its courtly train!

The lily with the sprinkled dots,
    Brands of the noontide beam;
The cardinal and the blood-red spots—
    Its double in the stream,

As if some wounded eagle's breast
    Slow throbbing o'er the plain,
Had left its airy path impressed
    In drops of scarlet rain.

And hark! and hark! the woodland rings;
    There thrilled the thrush's soul;

And look! and look! those lightning wings—
    The fire-plumed oriole!

Above the hen-hawk swims and swoops,
    Flung from the bright blue sky;
Below, the robin hops, and whoops
    His little Indian cry.

The beetle on the wave has brought
    A pattern all his own,
Shaped like the razor-breasted yacht
    To England not unknown.

Beauty runs virgin in the woods,
    Robed in her rustic green,
And oft a longing thought intrudes
    As if we nought have seen.

Her every fingers, every joint,
    Ringed with some golden line;
Poet whom Nature did anoint!
    Had our young home been thine.

Yet think not so; old England's blood
    Runs warm in English veins,
But wafted o'er the icy flood
    Its better life remains;

Our children know each wild-wood smell,
    The bayberry and the fern;
The man who does not know them well,
    Is all too old to learn.

Be patient; Love has long been grown;
    Ambition waxes strong;
And Heaven is asking time alone
    To mould a child of song.

When fate draws forth the mystic lot
  The chosen bard that calls,
No eye will be upon the spot
  Where the bright token falls.

Perchance the blue Atlantic's brink,
  The broad Ohio's gleam,
Or where the panther stoops to drink
  Of wild Missouri's stream :

Where winter clasps with glittering ice
  Katahdin's silver chains,
Or Georgia's flowery paradise
  Unfolds its blushing plains :

But know that none of ancient earth
  Can bring the sacred fire ;
He drinks the wave of Western birth
  That rules the Western lyre !

V.

YOUNG LADIES' INSTITUTE POEM.

Character of the Institute—Visited by John Quincy Adams—Graduating Exercises in 1849—Speech by Ex-President John Tyler—Speech and Poem by Oliver Wendell Holmes.

WE have already spoken of the Pittsfield, afterward the Maplewood, Young Ladies' Institute in connection with the Berkshire Jubilee dinner which was given upon its grounds. It was founded in 1841 by Rev. Wellington H. Tyler, a man of unlimited energy and spirit in his undertaking. In 1849 it had attained an enviable position among American institutions for the higher education of young women, and the addresses, poems, and like exercises at its graduating anniversaries would have done honor to any college commencement day. We are about to speak of these exercises in 1849, when Dr. Holmes took part in them; but the story of that occasion will derive interest from the relation of an incident in the annals of the institution six years before.

In the summer of 1843 the venerable ex-

President John Quincy Adams made a tour through the principal towns of Canada and northern New York, which was a continual series of remarkable ovations in which all classes and all parties united. On his way home, he was formally invited to Pittsfield, where the people of the town gave him a brilliant reception, in the course of which he made several characteristic speeches. At the public dinner he gave this toast: "The hills of Berkshire; the vales of Berkshire; the men of Berkshire; but, above all, the women of Berkshire."

Then the omnibus in which the young ladies were accustomed to ride conveyed him, with the officers of the day, to the Institute grounds, which had been adorned with rich evergreen arches and other decorations. Having been appropriately welcomed, "he addressed the members of the Institute in the most feeling and happy manner." He said that during the past month he had met with many kind receptions and tokens of regard from every rank, party, age, and profession, not only in a neighboring State, but in Canada. Yet in all, he had witnessed nothing so gratifying and interesting to him as the scene now before him. So many blooming countenances! He loved to look upon them—he should be happy to grasp their hands; and their voices, too, he should delight to hear; for these, he doubted not, were full of the sweetest melody. He saw before him those who reminded him of the happiest relations of his life—the relations of wife, mother, sister, daughter, and grand-daughter. It was these very relations that were impelling him this moment on his way, and drawing him with resistless power to his home. And, if he seemed to be breaking away from them, it was only that he might meet a wife, a daughter, and a grand-daughter of the same age as many he saw before him.

Then, after the singing of a hymn and warm hand-grasping, the venerable statesman and the blooming school-girls parted; but with memories of the day that could never fade.

That was a red-letter day for the Institute; and another like it came six years later. At the graduating exercises of 1849, the report of the examining committee was written and read by Rev. Dr. Henry Neill, of Lenox, an eloquent preacher and the author of some works distinguished for elegant scholarship, and the address was delivered by Rev. Dr. Brainerd, of New York.

Among the guests that summer at the Broadhall boarding-house was ex-President John Tyler, who, whatever politicians thought, seemed to enjoy keenly the relief afforded by his transfer from a not excessively agreeable official life at Washington to one of ease and independence, amid Berkshire scenery in the company of his recently wedded wife: a woman of brilliant wit, much culture, pleasing manners, and withal evidently devoted to her equally devoted husband, who, moreover, did not lack the society of friends whose friendship was to be prized, among his fellow-boarders and others in Berkshire, including Dr. Holmes. We venture to guess that there were pleasant passages of wit between the great humorist and Mrs. Tyler, who was nothing loath to such encounters. President Tyler attended the anniversary of the Young Ladies' Institute, and, after the more formal exercises, made, in response to the call of the principal, a most genial and pleasing address, from which we quote one paragraph:

"Is there any expression in language that so thrills the heart-strings as that of our 'mother'? She who gave direction to our early ideas, who first caused us to raise our little hands and eyes in prayer to the throne of the Most High; and shall her daughters be denied admission to those portals which open to a knowledge of the deep mysteries of nature and science? I am most happy to know that those portals are no longer closed, but are broadly and widely opened."

He then expressed an earnest hope for the success of the Institute and the prosperity of its teachers and trustees.

The principal, then, with a few complimentary remarks, called upon Dr. Holmes, who responded with the following poem and prefatory remarks:

"If it were any other place than Pittsfield, and if the occasion were any other than this which has called us together, I should certainly be unwilling to present myself before this audience after the exercises to which we have just listened. But the place has so many claims upon me, connected as it is with my most cherished recollections and my brightest hopes, and the occasion is one so capable of unsealing the lips of the dumb, and kindling light in the eyes of the blind, that I cannot refuse to follow my impulse against my judgment. After the interesting address which you have heard, the full and most satisfactory report of the committee, and the eloquent remarks of our distinguished visitor, it would ill become me to occupy your time with any attempts at expatiation on those subjects which naturally present themselves, but which have already been so well treated and so vividly illustrated. Let me rather, instead of toiling through an unnecessary series of phrases, and bowing myself out in a finished peroration, have recourse to an artifice under cover of which I have sometimes retreated from dangerous positions, like that which I now occupy.

"You have heard some allusions made to the

strains of a music-box, which, if it is wound up, plays out its single tune, and then subsides into mute companionship. There is another kind of music, which, as some think, is occasionally not disagreeable; and of which I mean to give you a most brief and compendious specimen. You must not think you are to have a symphony on the organ or a sonata from the piano; one little tinkling tune is all that will be played to you, and then the box will shut up, and you are to say no more about it.

"I will read you a few lines from a scrap of paper which, as you see, I have kept artfully concealed about my person.

A Vision of Life.

The well-known weakness of the rhyming race
Is to be ready in and out of place;
No bashful glow, no timid begging off,
No sudden hoarseness, no discordant cough
(Those coy excuses which your singers plead,
When faintly uttering: "No, I can't, indeed")
Impedes your rhymester in his prompt career.
Give him but hint; and *won't* the muse appear?

So, without blushing, when they asked, I came—
I whom the plough-share, not the quill, should claim—
The rural nymphs that on my labors smile
May mend my fence, but cannot mend my style.
The wingèd horse disdains my steady team,
And teeming fancy must forget to dream.
I harrow fields and not the hearts of men;
Pigs, and not poems, claim my humble pen.

And thus to enter on so new a stage,
With the fair critics of this captious age
Might lead a sceptic to the rude surmise
That cits, turned rustics, are not overwise;
Or the bright verdure of the pastoral scene
Had changed my hue, and made me very green.

A few brief words that, fading as they fall,
Like the green garlands of a festal hall,
May lend one glow, one breath of fragrance pour,
Ere swept ungathered from the silent floor.
Such is my offering for your festal day;
These sprigs of rhyme; this metrical boquet.

O, my sweet sisters—let me steal the name
Nearest to love and most remote from blame—
How brief an hour of fellowship ensures
The heart's best homage at a shrine like yours.
As o'er your band our kindling glances fall,
It seems a life-time since I've known you all!
Yet in each face where youthful graces blend
Our partial memory still revives a friend;
The forms once loved, the features once adored,
In her new picture nature has restored.

Those golden ringlets, rippling as they flow,
We wreathed with blossoms many years ago.
Seasons have wasted; but, remembered yet,
There gleams the lily through those braids of jet.
Cheeks that have faded worn by slow decay
Have caught new blushes from the morning's ray.
That simple ribbon, crossed upon the breast,
Wakes a poor heart that sobbed itself to rest;
Aye, thus she wore it; tell me not she died,
With that fair phantom floating by my side,

'Tis as of old: why ask the vision's name?
All, to the white robe's folding, is the same;
And there, unconscious of a hundred snows,
On that white bosom burns the self-same rose.

Oh, dear illusion, how thy magic power
Works with two charms—a maiden and a flower!
Then blame me not if, lost in memory's dream,
I cheat your hopes of some expansive theme.

When the pale star-light fills the evening dim,
A misty mantle folds our river's brim.
In those white wreaths, how oft the wanderer sees
Half real shapes, the playthings of the breeze.
While every image in the darkening tide
Fades from its breast, unformed and undescribed.
Thus, while I stand among your starry train,
My gathering fancies turn to mist again.
O'er time's dark wave aerial shadows play,
But all the living landscape melts away.

VI.

THE PLOUGHMAN.

Genesis of the Berkshire Agricultural Society—Elkanah Watson—Major Thomas Melville—John Quincy Adams upon Agricultural Oratory—The Picturesque First Cattle Show—How Women Received Their Premiums—About Ploughing Matches—Cattle Shows of 1849 and 1851—Dr. Holmes' Ploughing Match Report—His Poem, The Ploughman.

THE Agricultural Societies, of which almost every county in the Union and in Canada boasts at least one, still, as of old, furnish their peoples, in their autumnal cattle-shows and fairs, with gala days strikingly unlike any others. Most of them retain in some good degree the quaint provincial features which gave them irresistible attractions for country folk, and a singular charm for those familiar with the wide world's great spectacular festivals. In spite of "improvements"—which, whether they improve or not, do certainly innovate—the fandangos, the merry-go-rounds, the rude side-shows, the ruder oyster booths, the sweet-cider barrels, and all that used to delight what "Josh

Billings," and other county-wags before him, were wont to call "the kritter-look-krowd," still hold their own pretty well. Still, every fall, more or less competent orators dilate upon the historic, social, and economical aspects of the organizations they address, with more or less knowledge of what they are talking about. The practice of selecting agricultural orators for other reasons than their knowledge of agriculture has come down to us from the good old times. People, as a mass, always did, and always will, run to see and hear live governors, and live lions of any species. They draw. For draft purposes they easily take the first cattle-show premiums even over elephants. John Quincy Adams, however, did not favor their use. In a speech at Pittsfield, he mentioned that he had received several invitations to address agricultural societies, one of them from the "Old Berkshire," asking him to speak at its coming anniversary. "But," said he, "think of my coming to Berkshire to teach agriculture! I am no farmer: why, in all my life, I have not been at home long enough to become a proficient in it, and I believe with "Poor Richard," that

"'He who by the plough would thrive
Himself must either hold or drive.'"

But then Mr. Adams would have been very likely to disapprove many things now as strongly intrenched in popular favor as the Leo-Hunter craze of the agricultural societies is. And the societies continue to flourish in spite of all fault-finding critics. Something, indeed, of the picturesque and poetic coloring that gave beauty to the quaintness of their autumnal gatherings has faded since the times when William Cullen Bryant and Oliver Wendell Holmes were among their poets laureate; but not all. They are not yet entirely untinted of their old fascinating hues. This is especially true of the "Ancient and Honorable" Berkshire Agricultural Society—the parent of them all. The dominant peculiarities, which this institution transmitted to all its widespread progeny, were the fruit of much culture and knowledge of the world, gained partly in American cities, but much more largely in Europe; and applied to a secluded but intelligent and ambitious community. Elkanah Watson, the founder of the society, had opportunities in his youth to closely observe men and affairs during the Revolution, and to acquire something of its spirit; but, coming of age in 1779, he went to France, where he was engaged until 1784 in mercantile business that called for extensive travel in that country, as well as in Holland, Belgium, and Great Britain. Returning to America, he made his home in Albany, where, associated with several patriotic and public-spirited statesmen in plans for the good of the country, he became particularly interested in their efforts, and those of the New York State Agricultural Society, for the improvement of American wools,—which sadly needed improvement—by the importation of the best Spanish breeds of sheep, purchased in the markets thrown open by the wars of Napoleon. In 1807, he removed to Pittsfield, succeeding Henry Van Schaack on the Broadhall estate. Here he remembered what he had seen of festal and oratorical agricultural fairs in France, and of the less showy solid cattle-shows of England; and also that the New York State Society had recommended county societies and shows. These memories, together with the favorable position he occupied at Pittsfield, naturally inspired him with the idea which culminated four years later —after a world of effort on his part—in the establishment of the Berkshire Society for the Promotion of Agriculture and Manufactures. In 1814 he was succeeded in its presidency by Maj. Thomas Melville, who, when Mr. Watson returned to Albany in 1816, also succeeded him in the Broadhall property. He was an uncle of Herman Melville and son of the Maj. Thomas Melville who was one of the Boston Tea-Party of 1773, and, in his extreme old age, became the original of Dr. Holmes' "Last Leaf." The younger Major Melville passed much of his early life in France, where he had an interesting and romantic experience, and married a lady of family. He returned in season to be made commandant, with the rank of major, of the Pittsfield cantonment, and commissioner for the purchase of army supplies, a position which enabled him to speedily learn much of Berkshire farmers and their husbandry.

This happy combination, in the first two presidents of the Agricultural Society, of practical local knowledge, with tastes cultivated and thoughts quickened by energetic lives and wide observation abroad, all stimulated by patriotism enhanced by the war, together with Mr. Watson's inventive imagination and liberal purse, had its natural fruit in a community ordinarily distinguished for plain common sense and homely every-day labors; but which many instances show to have been extremely susceptible of incitement to enthusiasm when its love of country was properly appealed to. And a burning desire to free America from dependence upon British looms was a conspicuous, and indeed the primal, motive of the founders of the Berkshire Society for the promotion of agriculture and manufactures.

Pre-existing associations had exerted themselves zealously and accomplished something in this direction; but their members were, for the most part, men actively and deeply engaged in business, politics, or society. They held their meetings in metropolitan centers and worked, or sought to work, rather upon than among and with the country farmers. Thus they failed to obtain any strong hold upon the popular heart, and accomplished comparatively little in elevating farmers as a class intellectually, socially, or even in capacity for their own everyday calling. They created no great holiday for the people, no fellowship in the farmer's craft; and thus they missed the most potent means for raising American husbandry to a higher plane. "They depended," said Mr. Watson, "too much upon type, and did not address the interest and the sentiment of the people." Their approaches were too direct. They sought to influence their humbler fellows almost solely through the cold medium of the press; neglecting appeals to the imagination, to social sentiment, and to that fondness for pageantry which characterized the times. All this the founders of the Berkshire Society reversed; so molding it that in a few years its example inaugurated a new era in American agricultural life. This it effected through its annual cattle-shows and fairs.

The cattle-show, which was the germ of a class that has so increased and multiplied that its scions now flourish in every corner of the land, was held, under a call from twenty-six influential Berkshire farmers, in 1810, around the tall old elm which then stood in solitary grandeur on the village green that is now known as the Pittsfield Park. Although this show was little more than a display of cattle and sheep, followed by an address from Mr. Watson, it excited a wide interest, particularly in New England and New York. At home it created the Berkshire Agricultural Society, under whose auspices and control the second show and fair was held on the last Tuesday and Wednesday of September, 1811. This is the occasion to which Pittsfield traditions revert with unlimited pride; although some of the features of the show afterward the most popular were not yet introduced.

Two of Berkshire's most glorious September days blessed the young festival with an atmosphere at once genial and bracing. An unclouded but not torrid sun, and foliage not yet tinged with any hectic flush; all that Nature's ministers can offer in provision for the most unalloyed enjoyment of whatever of pleasure or interest man may prepare for enjoyment. The streets and Park square early took on the lively aspect that subsequent cattle-shows made familiar. People from the country round about, in all sorts of vehicles from a "one-horse shay" to a farm-wagon, began, before the rising of the sun, to pour into town, mixed with herds of cattle, sheep in wagons or in flocks, a few swine, and some mechanical inventions. Immediately around the tall elm, there was an inclosure for the live-stock entered for premium. The remaining space and the neighboring streets were soon thronged with an excited, expectant crowd: "many of them females,"—although the features which afterward made the festival of special interest to them were wanting. Booths for the sale of refreshments and Yankee notions had sprung up like mushrooms, after the fashion of the then familiar militia muster-fields. The committee had announced that "innocent amusements would be permitted," and enterprising genius provided a plenty. Chief among them was the fandango, or, as they styled it, the "aerial phaeton," whose dizzy pleasures have never since that day failed the lads and lasses who resort to cattle-shows. Then "the first elephant ever brought to America" gave the country folk their first chance to see "that remarkable creature," except in a cant metaphorical sense.

The procedings and pageants of the occasion were all unique and "telling;" but the procession was its crowning glory. Mr. Watson, in his diary, calls it "splendid, novel, and imposing beyond anything of the kind ever before exhibited in America." First came the Pittsfield band, whose music is described as inspiriting and creditable. Then followed sixty yoke of prime oxen, the oxen being driven and the plow held by the two oldest farmers in the town, whose plowing of its soil dated back to a time when it could only be done side by side with a musket, and under the near protection of log forts which these same old farmers had themselves built. Next came a broad platform drawn by oxen, bearing a broadcloth-handloom with a flying shuttle and a spinning-jenny of forty spindles, both machines kept in operation by skillful workmen; one of them, a remarkably fine-looking Englishman, wearing the costume of Dr. Holmes' "Last Leaf," which had even then almost passed from common wear. In this case it was entirely black, but decorated with an abundance of bright-colored ribbons or "favors." The next broad platform was drawn by horses—a prophecy of the coming change in rural motive power. It was in the nature of a triumphal car for what Berkshire had already achieved in manufactures; exhibiting rolls of broadcloth, bolts of sail-duck, handsome rose-blankets, leather, muskets, drums, anchors, and tall clocks like that which then stood in the hall stairway of the Gold mansion awaiting the coming of fame. The last division was composed of the officers and members of the society, their hats decorated with heads of wheat, and carrying a banner with a plow on one side and a sheaf of wheat on the reverse.

This display made an impression upon the people of the county which has never been effaced, but has been handed down to this day in the traditions of its old families so vividly that to have heard it in youth at the family fireside answers very well for a patent of county rank. The report of this cattle-show went far and wide, like that of the Berkshire Jubilee, but it had far more practical and permanent results; which were increased as new attractions were added to the programme of the festival. The first of these additions was effected by inducing the women of the county to take a personal part in the show. Mr. Watson had to exert all his ingenuity, and call in the aid of his wife, to overcome their native shy timidity; but he succeeded, and their display of household manufactures, fancy articles, dairy products, and the like, always thronged the halls in which they were exhibited with admiring crowds. The quilt that grandmother sent to the show in her young life and the silver bowl that grandfather's choice oxen won him are precious relics in old Berkshire families wherever time may have scattered them. A Virginian letter-writer, in 1822, thus described the scene when the premiums awarded to women were delivered.

"The president from the pulpit, immediately after the address, announced: 'As premiums are proclaimed for females they will please rise in their places, and the chief marshal will deliver to each her premium and certificate of honorable testimony.' The instant the name of the successful candidate was announced, the eyes of an exhilarated audience were flying in every direction, impelled by the strongest curiosity to see the fortunate blushing female, with downcast eyes, raising both her hands, as the marshal approached; with one to receive her premium, with the other her certificate. The effect cannot be described. It must be seen to be realized."

Strangely enough, the plowing match was not introduced until 1818, when it at once became the most exhilarating feature of the festival; receiving, as a competitive exhibition, the attention, and exciting the interest which have since, in a very large degree, been usurped by the then unknown "agricultural horse-trot;" as some think, not greatly to the advantage of agriculture. In the good old plowing-match times, at an appointed hour, the trial took place in a previously announced level and convenient field; to which the whole "kritter-look-krowd" repaired, eager with the liveliest anticipations. And they were never disappointed; for the contests were invariably precisely like that which

Dr. Holmes has pictured to the life in his poem of "The Ploughman;" a piece of word-painting as accurate as it is vivid.

At the first plowing match, the first premium was taken by Major Melville's ploughman; time, thirty-nine minutes. His competitors declared that his success was due to a superior iron plow which the major had just received from Boston. The curious in such matters may still see it in the historical cabinet of the Berkshire Athenæum, and judge its merits for themselves. It looks as though good work might be done with it rapidly.

Dr. Holmes read his admirable poem, "The Ploughman," in 1849. In 1852 a description of the cattle-show of 1851 was published, from which we take a couple of descriptive paragraphs.

"The festival of all festivals, the two days for which, in the opinion of our rural population, all other days in the round year were made, are those of the cattle-show and fair of the County Agricultural Society. Thanksgiving's grateful rest comes after. This is the shining goal of the year's race. Dreaming of a silver cup, or at least "honorable mention," the farmer tills his soil, tends his flocks and herds, and is careful for many things in sunshine and storm. For the same momentous occasion the busy fingers of his wife and daughters are plied, while in the dairy, cleanliest receptacles are filled with balls of golden-hued butter and cylinders of odorous cheese. In chambers, too, quaintly variegated needleworks bud and blossom, and snowy webs issue from the antique loom.

Nor do the taper fingers of more dainty ladies disdain to contend for the silver spoons; while retired gentlemen of fortune take a notable pride in the display of luscious fruits and mammoth vegetables.

The village beaux prize the day as an occasion for the display of superior gallantry; and the village magnates aspire to the offices in the gift of the society as no small distinctions in themselves, and possibly—pardon the suspicion —as stepping-stones to more substantial honors. Few among us but are at least amateurs in agriculture; so that when the great festival of Ceres approaches, our mountain Microcosmos is all agog with excitement. The country around is in a ferment of preparation; now is the harvest of the village tailors; now the paraphernalia of the village belles is cunningly renovated for conquest. . . . On the bright and beautiful morning of the second day of the fair, we again sallied forth in quest of adventure. The streets were thronged with all sorts of people, seemingly like ourselves, with no very definite notion of what they were after:

"Like a flock of sheep,
Not knowing and not caring whither
They come or go—so that they fool together."

My brain is mazed with the memory of that motley crowd. The delegate from Peacham, with gingerbread under one arm and "umbrell" under the other, jostled the gloved and caned exquisite from Broadway; and the traveler who could compare this with the great fairs of Europe was favored with the opinion of the youth whose eyes had hardly peeped over the Berkshire Hills—and it may be was wise enough to learn something from it. Here and there, men whose names were known the world over in literature or politics went about—moralizing, perhaps; or, much more likely, watching that most animating portion of the scene:

"The lassies with sly eyes,
And the smile settling in their sun-flecked cheeks,
Like bloom upon the mellow apricot."

One of these famous people was Dr. Holmes, whom the writer then first saw, as he was leading from booth to booth, and from side-show to side-show, a little boy—very likely, the since gallant captain and learned judge. At the cattle-show, two years before this, Dr. Holmes was chairman of the committee on the plowing-match, being probably induced to accept that position, and write the poem to which it led, by his personal friendship for Hon. Ensign H. Kellogg, who was secretary and actuary of the society.

The oral exercises of the festival were held in the old church of 1791, in which at two cattle-shows, years before, Bryant had listened to the singing of odes written for them by himself; and which had been the theater of many memorable scenes and events. The cattle-show exercises always filled it to its full capacity with such an audience as may be imagined from what has been said. It could not be more than filled on this occasion, but there was a much larger sprinkling than usual of the more cultivated class; a hint of the coming treat having passed from mouth to mouth among them. When the report of the plowing-match committee was called for, there was a storm of applause; Dr. Holmes' Jubilee poem being still fresh in the minds of the people. After gracefully recognizing it by a bow, he mounted halfway up the old-fashioned high pulpit stairs and, turning to the audience, read his report; of which we give below what is of permanent interest, and the poem it introduces; a poem which all critics now class as one of the finest georgics in the whole range of modern poetry; and which some of the best hold to be without a rival.

REPORT.

The committee on the plowing-match are fully sensible of the dignity and importance of the office entrusted to their judgment. To decide upon the comparative merits of so many excellent specimens of agricultural art is a most delicate, responsible, and honorable duty.

The plough is a very ancient implement. It is written in the English language p-l-o-u-g-h, and, by the association of free and independent spellers, p-l-o-w. It may be remarked that the same gentlemen can, by a similar process, turn their coughs into cows; which would be the cheapest mode of raising live stock, although it is to be feared that they (referring to the cows) would prove but low-bred animals. Some have derived the English word plough from the Greek *ploutos*, the wealth which comes from the former suggesting its resemblance to the latter. But such resemblances between different languages may be carried too far: as for example, if a man should trace the name of the Altamaha to the circumstance that the first settlers were all tomahawked on the margin of that river.

Time and experience have sanctioned the custom of putting only plain, practical men upon this committee. Were it not so, the most awkward blunders would be constantly occurring. The inhabitants of our cities, who visit the country during the fine season, would find themselves quite at a loss if an overstrained politeness should place them in this position. Imagine a trader, or a professional man, from the capital of the State, unexpectedly called upon to act in rural matters. Plough-shares are to him shares that pay no dividends. A coulter, he supposes, has something to do with a horse. His notions of stock were obtained in Faneuil Hall market, where the cattle looked funnily enough, to be sure, compared with the living originals. He knows, it is true, that there is a difference in cattle, and would tell you that he prefers the sirloin breed. His children are equally unenlightened; they know no more of the poultry-yard than what they have learned by having the chicken-pox, and playing on a Turkey carpet. Their small knowledge of wool-growing is lam(b)entable.

The history of one of these summer-visitors shows how imperfect is his rural education. He no sooner establishes himself in the country than he begins a series of experiments. He tries to drain a marsh, but only succeeds in draining his own pockets. He offers to pay for carting off a compost heap; but is informed that it consists of corn and potatoes in an unfinished state. He sows abundantly, but reaps little or nothing, except with the implement which he uses in shaving; a process which is frequently performed for him by other people, though he pays no barber's bill. He builds a wire-fence and paints it green, so that nobody can see it. But he forgets to order a pair of spectacles apiece for his cows, who, taking offense at something else, take his fence in addition, and make an invisible one of it sure enough. And, finally, having bought a machine to chop fodder, which chops off a good slice of his dividends, and two or three children's fingers, he concludes that, instead of cutting feed, he will cut farming; and so sells out to one of those plain, practical farmers, such as you have honored by placing them on your committee; whose pockets are not so full when he starts, but have fewer holes and not so many fingers in them.

It must have been one of these practical men whose love of his pursuits led him to send in to the committee the following lines, which it is hoped will be accepted as a grateful tribute to the noble art whose successful champions are now to be named and rewarded.

Dr. Holmes then read " The Ploughman."

THE PLOUGHMAN.

Clear the brown path to meet his coulter's gleam!
Lo! on he comes behind his smoking team,
With toil's bright dew-drops on his sunburnt brow,
The lord of earth, the hero of the plough!

THE POET AMONG THE HILLS.

First in the field before the reddening sun,
Last in the shadows when the day is done,
Line after line, along the bursting sod,
Marks the broad acres where his feet have trod;
Still where he treads, the stubborn clods divide,
The smooth, fresh furrow opens deep and wide;
Matted and dense the tangled turf upheaves,
Mellow and dark the ridgy cornfield cleaves;
Up the steep hillside, where the laboring train
Slants the long track that scores the level plain;
Through the moist valley, clogged with oozing clay,
The patient convoy breaks its destined way;
At every turn the loosening chains resound,
The swinging ploughshare circles glistening round,
Till the wide field one billowy waste appears
And wearied hands unbind the panting steers.

These are the hands whose sturdy labor brings
The peasant's food, the golden pomp of kings;
This is the page whose letters shall be seen
Changed by the sun to words of living green;
This is the scholar, whose immortal pen
Spells the first lesson hunger taught to men;
These are the lines, oh, Heaven-commanded toil,
That fill thy deed—thy charter of the soil!

O, gracious Mother, whose benignant breast
Wakes us to life, and lulls us all to rest,
How sweet thy features, kind to every clime,
Mock with their smile the wrinkled front of time!
We stain thy flowers,—they blossom o'er the dead;
We rend thy bosom, and it gives us bread;
O'er the red field that trampling strife has torn,
Waves the green plumage of thy tasselled corn;
Our maddening conflicts scar thy fairest plain,
Still thy soft answer is the growing grain.

Yet, O our Mother, while uncounted charms
Round the fresh clasp of thine embracing arms,
Let not our virtues in thy love decay,
And thy fond sweetness waste our strength away.

No! by these hills, whose banners now displayed
In blazing cohorts Autumn has arrayed;
By you twin crests, amid the sinking sphere,
Last to dissolve and first to reappear;
By these fair plains the mountain circle screens
And feeds in silence from its dark ravines,
True to their homes, these faithful arms shall toil
To crown with peace their own untainted soil;
And true to God, to freedom and mankind,
If her chained bandogs Faction shall unbind,
These stately forms, that bending even now,
Bowed their strong manhood to the humble plough,
Shall rise erect, the guardians of the land,
The same stern iron in the same right hand,
Till Greylock thunders to the setting sun,
"The sword has rescued what the ploughshare won."

The reader familiar with Dr. Holmes' poetry may perhaps observe that some of the lines in the latter part of the above poem vary somewhat from the corresponding ones in "The Ploughman" as given in the published collections of the author's works. This is due to the fact that we give the poem as part of his cattle-show report on the plowing match of 1849; and print it as recorded in that connection. But, certainly and without a peradventure, every reader will observe in the grand poetry of these closing lines, the grander prophecy that was grandly fulfilled many years after it was pronounced from the pulpit-stairs of the old meeting-house of patriotic associations.

VII.

PITTSFIELD CEMETERY DEDICATION POEM.

Description of Cemetery Grounds—Previous Burial-Grounds—Dedication Exercises—Rev. Dr. Neill's Address Quoted—Dr. Holmes and Wendell Phillips—The Poem.

THE Pittsfield Rural Cemetery is one of the most beautiful and interesting places of repose for a city's dead. There are few so well fitted to soothe the mourner at his loved one's grave, as this where he finds it amid noble and gently pleasing natural scenery, developed but undisturbed by art. The visiting stranger also keenly enjoys these beauties, less veiled for him with saddened thought; and with the deeper interest if he is able to invest it with the historic associations that of right belong to it.

Previous to the year 1850, the encroachments of the living upon the resting-places—or what should have been the resting-places—of Pittsfield's dead, and the consequent removal of their ashes from one burial-ground to another, excited painful and indignant feeling in hearts to which those ashes were endeared by memory;

and sense of a wrong near akin to sacrilege in many others. Circumstances in the early spring of 1850 so intensified this feeling that the town reversed its policy and ordered the purchase of a spacious and every way suitable site for a cemetery, a mile north of its central business square. In April, 1850, this property was conveyed in trust to a corporation charged with its preparation for the object of its purchase, and with its care and management for that object in perpetuity.

In an official report of this corporation the grounds which they received are thus described with perfect accuracy:

"Alternate woods and lawns vary the scene. The irregularity of its surface, now breaking away into gentle inclinations and rounded knolls, adds greatly to its attractions. Fine trees dot the landscape, rural sights meet the eye wherever it is turned. Hidden within the deep shade of the woods, the wanderer is shut out from the world; but as he emerges upon the uplands, the spires of the village, the quiet homesteads of the valley, and the distant mountains break upon him with a beauty almost enrapturing."

Dr. Horatio Stone, of New York, an artist of well-won national reputation for such work, was engaged to lay out these grounds and transform them from a beautiful natural park to a beautiful and well-arranged cemetery. Poet and sculptor, his fine taste and peculiar genius made the best possible use of the facilities which nature offered him for making the spot intrusted to him more lovely than he received it.

All summer long men and women of taste and feeling cheered and encouraged him by their visits and praises; among them Dr. Holmes, who thus had frequent opportunities to make studies of the superb and varied landscape for his coming poem.

As the fall approached, although Dr. Stone's plans had been but incompletely carried out, it was determined to dedicate the cemetery, and open it for use in accordance with an earnest desire of the people who were reluctant to lay their dead in burial-grounds soon to be abandoned. But, although much remained to be done, much had already been accomplished. Without trenching upon their wild-wood character, the groves had been rounded into grace, and freed from the unsightliness of decay and careless destruction. Man had restored to nature something of the symmetry of which his rude and hasty greed had robbed her. The waters of Onota flowed in a bold and rapid stream across the entrance of the cemetery; but some of them had been trained in a winding brook to a beautiful lawn where they spread into a pretty lakelet, to which Dr. Stone gave the name of St. John, the loving and beloved apostle of Christ; the consoler of the mourner. Miles of roads and paths wound in gentle curves through every part of the grounds; while along their western border one broad, straight avenue was prepared to receive its long vista of trees. Everywhere a beautiful present prophesied the more beautiful future.

Monday the 9th of September was fixed for the dedication, and even that choice week of all the year in Pittsfield never afforded a more perfect day. The procession which, early in the forenoon, moved from the park to the cemetery, was heterogeneous, but not in bad taste, as it forcibly represented the hold which the noble public work which called for it had taken upon the hearts of all classes of citizens. A platform for the speakers and the choir had been erected on the northern slope of Chapel Hill, opposite the south shore of the lakelet of St. John. And when the procession arrived, the whole population of the town seemed to be grouped around it. An elaborate program of exercises had been arranged and was perfectly carried out. It included addresses, prayers, and the singing of appropriate original odes. The dedicatory address was delivered by Rev. Dr. Henry Neill, of Lenox, and consisted chiefly of reasons why living men should institute memorials for the dead and make beautiful the spots consecrated to their rest and their memory; the argument being eloquently pressed and illustrated by exquisitely told instances from ancient and modern history. We quote the opening passage:

"Have we been persuaded—an assembly of the living—to look upon the very ground where we may sleep? Impelled by a desire to do honor to the dead, have we come within the precincts of a spot where every shadow seems now to deepen, and where the mountains point significantly to the skies? The sense of an unpaid tribute has summoned us from our homes. Affection in its reverence and depth of tenderness has longed to give itself expression in some outward, significant, and permanent form until it can no longer be denied. Out of the hearts of a large community the declaration at length has come, that the remains of departed worth shall hereafter find a safe retreat and pledges of remembrance, foretokening their recompense of a higher reward."

The dedicatory poem was then read by Dr. Holmes. Nowhere can the poem be so fully understood and enjoyed as here, where it first fell from the lips of its author in the presence of the landscape, and on the occasion, which inspired it. Nor can the varied charms of that landscape be in any other way so adequately appreciated as under the immediate interpretation of the verse which at once described them with the fidelity of a photograph, and gave them a soul with all a great poet's creative power. And yet that verse can never again thrill as it thrilled those who heard it pronounced in clear and silvery tones, in the grove on Chapel Hill, that superb and memorable September day of 1850.

Dr. Holmes is reported to have answered, when he was asked where Wendell Phillips got those marvelous tones that, like magic music, charmed the most hostile audience, that it was "at his mother's knee," or " in his mother's parlor"; but those who listened to his own voice, not ringing but flowing through the greenwood arches of Chapel Hill, will believe that the gift to both was from a common ancestry far back of that. There was much that day to give character to the solemn consecration of our cemetery; but the willing and sympathizing genius of Oliver Wendell Holmes embalmed it forever in immortal verse.

Dedicatory Poem.

Angel of Death! Extend thy silent reign!
Stretch thy dark sceptre o'er this new domain!
No sable car along the winding road
Has borne to earth its unresisting load;
No sudden mound has risen yet to show
Where the pale slumberer folds his arms below;

No marble gleams to bid his memory live
In the brief lines that hurrying Time can give;
Yet, O Destroyer! From thy shrouded throne
Look on our gift; this realm is all thine own!
Fair is the scene; its sweetness oft beguiled
From their dim paths the children of the wild;
The dark-haired maiden loved its grassy dells,
The feathered warrior claimed its wooded swells,
Still on its slopes the ploughman's ridges show
The pointed flints that left his fatal bow,
Chipped with rough art and slow barbarian toil, —
Last of his wrecks that strews the alien soil!
Here spread the fields that waved their ripened store
Till the brown arms of Labor held no more;
The scythe's broad meadow with its dusky blush;
The sickle's harvest with its velvet flush;
The green-haired maize, her silken tresses laid,
In soft luxuriance, on her harsh brocade;
The gourd that swells beneath her tossing plume;
The coarser wheat that rolls in lakes of bloom, —
Its coral stems and milk-white flowers alive
With the wide murmurs of the scattered hive;
Here glowed the apple with the pencilled streak
Of morning painted on its southern cheek;
The pear's long necklace strung with golden drops,
Arched, like the banian, o'er its pillared props;
Here crept the growths that paid the laborer's care
With the cheap luxuries wealth consents to spare;
Here sprang the healing herbs which could not save
The hand that reared them from the neighboring
    grave.

Yet all its varied charms, forever free
From task and tribute, Labor yields to thee;
No more when April sheds her fitful rain
The sower's hand shall cast its flying grain;

No more when Autumn strews the flaming leaves
The reaper's band shall gird its yellow sheaves;
For thee alike the circling seasons flow
Till the first blossoms heave the latest snow.
In the stiff clod below the whirling drifts,
In the loose soil the springing herbage lifts,
In the hot dust beneath the parching weeds
Life's wilting flower shall drop its shrivelled seeds;
Its germ entranced in thy unbreathing sleep
Till what thou sowest mightier angels reap!

Spirit of Beauty! Let thy graces blend
With loveliest Nature all that Art can lend.
Come from the bowers where Summer's life-blood flows
Through the red lips of June's half-open rose,
Dressed in bright hues, the loving sunshine's dower;
For tranquil Nature owns no mourning flower.
Come from the forest where the beech's screen
Bars the fierce noonbeam with its flakes of green;
Stay the rude axe that bares the shadowy plains,
Stanch the deep wound that dries the maple's veins.
Come with the stream whose silver-braided rills
Fling their unclasping bracelets from the hills,
Till in one gleam, beneath the forest's wings,
Melts the white glitter of a hundred springs.

Come from the steeps where look majestic forth
From their twin thrones the Giants of the North
On the huge shapes that crouching at their knees,
Stretch their broad shoulders, rough with shaggy trees.
Through the wide waste of ether, not in vain
Their softened gaze shall reach our distant plain;
There, while the mourner turns his aching eyes
On the blue mounds that print the bluer skies,
Nature shall whisper that the fading view
Of mightiest grief may wear a heavenly hue.

Cherub of Wisdom! Let thy marble page
Leave its sad lesson, new to every age;
Teach us to live, not grudging every breath
To the chill winds that waft us on to death,
But ruling calmly every pulse it warms
And tempering gently every word it forms.

Seraph of Love! In Heaven's adoring zone
Nearest of all around the central throne,
While with soft hands the pillowed turf we spread
That soon shall hold us in its dreamless bed,
With the low whisper—Who shall first be laid
In the dark chamber's yet unbroken shade?—
Let thy sweet radiance shine rekindled here,
And all we cherish grow more truly dear.
Here in the gates of Death's o'erhanging vault,
Oh, teach us kindness for our brother's fault;
Lay all our wrongs beneath this peaceful sod
And lead our hearts to Mercy and its God.

FATHER of all! In Death's relentless claim
We read thy mercy by its sterner name;
In the bright flower that decks the solemn bier
We see thy glory in its narrowed sphere;
In the deep lessons that affliction draws
We trace the curves of thy encircling laws;
In the long sigh that sets our spirits free
We own the love that calls us back to thee!

Through the hushed street, along the silent plain
The spectral future leads its mourning train,
Dark with the shadows of uncounted bands,
Where man's white lips and woman's wringing hands
Track the still burden, rolling slow before,
That love and kindness can protect no more;
The smiling babe that, called to mortal strife,
Shuts its meek eyes and drops its little life;

The drooping child that prays in vain to live,
And pleads for help its parent cannot give;
The pride of beauty stricken in its flower;
The strength of manhood broken in an hour;
Age in its weakness, bowed by toil and care,
Traced in sad lines beneath its silvered hair.
 The sun shall set, and heaven's resplendent spheres
Gild the smooth turf unhallowed yet by tears,
But ah, how soon the evening stars will shed
Their sleepless light around the slumbering dead!

 Take them, O Father, in immortal trust!
Ashes to ashes, dust to kindred dust,
Till the last angel rolls the stone away
And a new morning brings eternal day!

VIII.

THE NEW EDEN.

How the Poem Was Written.

THERE is a curious story connected with the writing of "The New Eden." The Berkshire Horticultural Society had a very pleasant anniversary dinner at Stockbridge, September 13, 1854, which was attended by persons of nice tastes from all parts of the county. Among them was Hon. Edward A. Newton, of Pittsfield, a gentleman of rare, varied, and fastidious culture. On his return, Mr. Newton, meeting a local editor, extolled without measure a poem which Dr. Holmes had read at the dinner, and urged the editor to procure it for publication; and he accordingly asked for it, although, knowing the money value of Dr. Holmes' verse, he had great doubts about obtaining it. But the poet, with his usual kindness—aided perhaps by a good word from his friend, Mr. Newton—readily consented to furnish the copy on three conditions: that he should have as many proofs and make as many alterations as he might please, and that, when the poem was ready, he should have a hundred copies handsomely printed on commercial note-paper. These terms would have been but trifling for the least considerable poem from Dr. Holmes' pen. They were eagerly accepted. He had sixteen proofs, and made so many alterations and additions that the completed poem—"The New Eden"—was more than double the length of that read at Stockbridge; while the slight infusion of humor that flavored it for the dinner-table had entirely disappeared.

It is only necessary to add by way of explanation, that in the summer of 1854 Berkshire County suffered from one of the most severe and prolonged droughts it ever knew. The poem portrays it with its author's invariable fidelity to Nature.

THE NEW EDEN.

Scarce could the parting ocean close,
  Seamed by the Mayflower's cleaving bow,
When o'er the rugged desert rose
  The waves that tracked the Pilgrim's plough.

Then sprang from many a rock-strewn field
  The rippling grass, the nodding grain,
Such growths as English meadows yield
  To scanty sun and frequent rain.

But when the fiery days were done,
  And Autumn brought his purple haze,
Then, kindling in the slanted sun,
  The hill-sides gleamed with golden maize.

Nor treat his homely gift with scorn
  Whose fading memory scarce can save
The hillocks where he sowed his corn,
  The mounds that mark his nameless grave.

The food was scant, the fruits were few:
  A red streak glistened here and there;
Perchance in statelier precincts grew
  Some stern old Puritanic pear.

Austere in taste, and tough at core
  Its unrelenting bulk was shed,
To ripen in the Pilgrim's store
  When all the summer sweets were fled.

Such was his lot, to front the storm
  With iron heart and marble brow,
Nor ripen till his earthly form
  Was cast from life's Autumnal bough.

But ever on the bleakest rock
  We bid the brightest beacon glow
And still upon the thorniest stock
  The sweetest roses love to blow.

So on our rude and wintry soil
  We feed the kindling flame of art,
And steal the tropic's blushing spoil
  To bloom on Nature's icy heart.

See how the softening Mother's breast
  Warms to her children's patient wiles,—
Her lips by loving Labor pressed
  Break in a thousand dimpling smiles,

From when the flushing bud of June
  Dawns with its first auroral hue,

Till shines the rounded harvest moon,
   And velvet dahlias drink the dew.

Nor these the only gifts she brings;
   Look where the laboring orchard groans,
And yields its beryl-threaded strings
   For chestnut burs and hemlock cones.

Dear though the shadowy maple be,
   And dearer still the whispering pine,
Dearest yon russet-laden tree
   Browned by the heavy rubbing kine!

There childhood flung its venturous stone,
   And boyhood tried its daring climb,
And though our summer birds have flown
   It blooms as in the olden time.

Nor be the Fleming's pride forgot,
   With swinging drops and drooping bells,
Freckled and splashed with streak and spot,
   On the warm-breasted, sloping swells;

Nor Persia's painted garden-queen,—
   Frail Houri of the trellised wall,—
Her deep-cleft bosom scarfed with green,—
   Fairest to see, and first to fall.

When man provoked his mortal doom,
   And Eden trembled as he fell,
When blossoms sighed their last perfume,
   And branches waved their long farewell,

One sucker crept beneath the gate,
   One seed was wafted o'er the wall,
One bough sustained his trembling weight;
   These left the garden—these were all.

And far o'er many a distant zone
  These wrecks of Eden still are flung:
The fruits that Paradise hath known
  Are still in earthly gardens hung.

Yes, by our own unstoried stream
  The pink-white apple-blossoms burst
That saw the young Euphrates gleam—
  That Gihon's circling waters nursed.

For us the ambrosial pear displays
  The wealth its arching branches hold,
Bathed by a hundred summery days
  In floods of mingling fire and gold.

And here, where beauty's cheek of flame
  With morning's earliest beam is fed,
The sunset-painted peach may claim
  To rival its celestial red.

What though in some unmoistened vale
  The summer leaf grow brown and sere,
Say, shall our star of promise fail
  That circles half the rolling sphere,

From beaches salt with bitter spray
  O'er prairies green with softest rain
And ridges bright with evening's ray
  To rocks that shade the stormless main?

If by our slender-threaded streams
  The blade and leaf and blossom die,
If drained by noon-tide's parching beams
  The milky veins of Nature dry,

See with her swelling bosom bare
  Yon wild-eyed Sister in the West,—

The ring of Empire round her hair,—
The Indian's wampum on her breast!

We saw the August sun descend
 Day after day with blood-red stain,
And the blue mountains dimly blend
 With smoke-wreaths from the burning plain;

Beneath the hot Sirocco's wings
 We sat and told the withering hours,
Till Heaven unsealed its azure springs,
 And bade them leap in flashing showers.

Yet in our Ishmael's thirst we knew
 The mercy of the Sovereign hand
Would pour the fountain's quickening dew
 To feed some harvest of the land.

No flaming swords of wrath surround
 Our second Garden of the Blest;
It spreads beyond its rocky bound
 It climbs Nevada's glittering crest.

God keep the tempter from its gate!
 God shield the children, lest they fall
From their stern fathers' free estate,
 Till Ocean is its only wall!

IX.

POEMS FOR LADIES' FAIR.

St. Stephen's Church Fair—A Lady's Raid on Dr. Holmes' Poetical Preserves — Camilla — Portia's Leaden Casket—What a Dollar Will Buy.

DURING his Pittsfield residence, Dr. Holmes was a constant attendant on St. Stephen's Church; and he took a genuine interest in the prosperity of the parish as it was indicated by the enlargement and improvement of its neat little gray-stone Gothic edifice—an interest that continued through life, as was pleasantly shown in a letter of 1893, warmly congratulating his long-time friend, Rev. Dr. Newton, the rector in that year, upon the completion of the large and beautiful church then just erected. Among other touching memories, it recalled the writer's attendance in the old church, to whose building he made a curious contribution, that is now to be described here. In 1855, St. Stephen's parishioners were even more than usually zealous. The ladies, as ever, were foremost in their zeal; and they made extraordinary preparations for a fair that is still brilliant in local society tradition. In their councils, they cast longing eyes toward the villa by the Housatonic. They had even the temerity to solicit a contribution from its master—not from his purse or his garden, which were open enough, but from his pen: something for the fair "post-office." He happened to be at the moment so pressed for time that he was compelled to plead preoccupation.

The committee were in despair. But Broadhall was then the home of Mr. and Mrs. J. R. Morewood; both among the most devoted St. Stephen's parishioners. Mrs Morewood had too wide acquaintance with literary lions to be daunted even by one so formidable as Dr. Holmes,—who did not become "Autocratic" until two years later. Perhaps, too, the lady had an inkling that his kind heart, and their common love for St. Stephen's would aid her pleading. At any rate, when she heard of the committee's disappointment she at once mounted her horse and, with a single aid-de-camp, dashed off to the villa by the Housatonic. There she presented her petition, and it almost goes without saying that it was granted by the promise of two poems for the post-office. Dr. Holmes, of course, escorted his fair besieger to the door; and in assisting her to remount her horse, being perhaps poetically nervous, he did not calculate with precise accuracy the amount of force necessary to place her gracefully in her seat. The saddle was, however, gained without a fall. But the poet, busy as he was, did not forget the incident, and when the fair postmistress received the two poems promised for her mail, there came also one for Mrs. Morewood, which described it with his never-failing grace, wit, and accuracy. We present it here.

CAMILLA.

The gray robe trailing round her feet,
    She smiled and took the slippered stirrup
(A smile as sparkling, rosy, sweet,
    As soda, drawn with strawberry syrup);—
Now, gallant, now! be strong and calm,—
    The graceful toilet is completed,—
Her foot is in thy hollowed palm—
    One little spring, and she is seated!

No foot-print on the grass was seen,
    The clover hardly bent beneath her,
I knew not if she pressed the green,
    Or floated over it in ether;
Why, such an airy, fairy thing
    Should carry ballast in her pocket,—
God bless me! If I help her spring
    She'll shoot up heavenward like a rocket.

Ah, fatal doubt! The sleepless power
    That chains the orbs of light together,
Bends on its stem the slenderest flower
    That lifts its plume from turf or heather;

Clasp, lady, clasp the bridle rein!
  The filly stands—hold hard upon her!
Twine fast those fingers in her mane,
  Or all is lost—excepting honor!

Earth stretched his arms to snatch his prize,
  The fairies shouted "Stand from under!"
The violets shut their purple eyes,
  The naked daisies stared in wonder;
One moment.——Seated in her pride,
  Those arms shall try in vain to win her;
"Earth claims her not," the fairies cried,
  "She has so little of it in her!"

The lady's raid on his poetic preserves, with its closing incident, reminded her classic host of Diana's light-footed messenger, Camilla, and probably of Pope's old familiar lines:

"When swift Camilla scours along the plain,
Flies o'er the unbending corn, and skims along the main."

The two other poems were inclosed in envelopes, inscribed with mottoes. These were disposed of in a raffle, the winner of the first prize selecting that of the two poems which pleased him, from the motto on the envelope.

PORTIA'S LEADEN CASKET.

Mrs. Ensign H. Kellogg drew the first prize and selected the envelope inscribed with the following

MOTTO.

Faith is the conquering Angel's crown;
Who hopes for grace must ask it;
Look shrewdly ere you lay me down;
I'm Portia's leaden casket.

The following verses were found within:

Fair lady, whosoe'er thou art,
  Turn this poor leaf with tenderest care
And—hush, O hush thy beating heart—
  The One thou lovest will be there!

Alas! not loved by thee alone,
  Thine idol, ever prone to range;
To-day, all thine, to-morrow flown,
  Frail thing that every hour may change.

Yet, when that truant course is done,
  If thy lost wanderer reappear,
Press to thy heart the only One
  That nought can make more truly dear!

Within this note was a slip of paper, with the following verses, inclosing a *one* dollar bill:

Fair lady, lift thine eyes and tell
  If this is not a truthful letter,
This is the one (1) thou lovest well
  And nought (0) can make thee love it better (10).

Though fickle, do not think it strange
  That such a friend is worth possessing,
For one that gold can never change,
  Is Heaven's own dearest earthly blessing.

What a Dollar Will Buy.

The second prize fell to Col. George S. Willis. The following was the

MOTTO.

If man, or boy, or dolt, or scholar
Will break this seal, he pays his dollar;
But if he reads a single minute,
He'll find *a dollar's worth* within it.

A DOLLAR'S WORTH.

Listen to me and I will try
To tell you what a dollar will buy.

A dollar will buy a Voter's conscience,
Or a book of "Fiftieth thousand" nonsense;

Or a ticket to hear a Prima Donna,
Or a fractional part of a statesman's honor;

It will buy a tree to sit in the shade of,
Or half the cotton a *tournure's* made of.

It will buy a glass of rum or gin
At a Deacon's store or a Temperance inn.

(The Deacon will show you how to mix it,
Or the Temperance Landlord stay and fix it.)

It will buy a painting at Burbank's hall
That will frighten the spiders from off the wall;

Or a dozen teaspoons of medium size,
That will do for an Agricultural prize.

It will buy four tickets to Barnum's show—
(Late firm of Pharaoh, Herod & Co.)
Or get you a paper that brings by mail
Its weekly "Original thrilling tale"—
Of which the essential striking plot
Is a daddy that's rich and a youth that's not,
Who seeking in vain for Papa's consent,
Runs off with his daughter—the poor old gent!
The Governor's savage; at last relents
And leaves them a million in cash and rents.

Or a Hair-wash, patent, and warranted too,
That will turn your whiskers from gray to blue,
And dye old three-score as good as new;
So that your wife will open her eyes
And treat you with coolness, and then surprise,
And at last, as you're sidling up to her,
Cry "I'll call my husband, you saucy cur!"

Or a monochrome landscape, done in an hour,
That looks like a ceiling stained in a shower;

Or a ride to Lenox through mire and clay,
Where you may see, through the livelong day,
Scores of women with couples of men
Trudging up hill—and down again.

This is what a dollar will do,
With many things as strange but true;
This very dollar I've got from you—
P. S. We shouldn't mind if you made it *two*.

Two or three of the hits in "A Dollar's Worth" do not fit quite so well as they did in 1855. Time has wrought many changes in forty years: but none to affect the victims of these verses so seriously that the reader cannot find somewhere some application for their wit.

The allusion to the paintings in Burbank's Hall is so local and dates so far back that it requires a little explanation. This hall, the largest in Pittsfield for years, was a very plain affair; but, on account of its size, it was used for all the purposes which, in a thriving New England village, call for such an audience-room. All the great lyceum orators of the day, including Dr. Holmes himself, spoke from its platform; and Fanny Kemble read Shakespeare on it to a thousand people. One day a hundred or more of the vilest daubs that ever pretended to be paintings were brought to it to be sold. It is a credit to Pittsfield that nobody would buy them, even for the value of their frames. Mr. Burbank, therefore, took the lot for his rent; and in 1855 they hung on the walls as a relief, if not an ornament, to their barrenness. What finally became of them we do not know. Perhaps they were in the wreck, when the hall itself crashed down under a weight of snow in 1861.

The sale of the two poems sent by Dr. Holmes to the Fair added twenty-five dollars to its receipts, which were applied to the cost of remodeling the church; so that the St. Stephen's of that time was the third Pittsfield house of worship to whose building the descendants of Col. Jacob Wendell contributed.

X.

L'ENVOI.

The Mountains and the Sea—Presentation from Dr. Holmes' Library to the Berkshire Athenæum—Hawthorne's Desk—Pittsfield Characters in Dr. Holmes' Novels—Good-By, Old Folks!

IF a multitude of witnesses will serve, all that the earlier pages of this volume advanced relative to the kindly feeling of Oliver Wendell Holmes for the mountain county of the Bay State, and particularly for the town of his summer home, has been made good; however imperfectly the argument founded upon their evidence may have been presented.

Still we may be permitted to add a few more words of similar import. And, again, they are mostly his own; being part of a Breakfast-Table Talk.

"I have lived by the sea-shore and by the mountains. No, I am not going to say which I like best. The one where your place is, is the best for you. But this difference there is: you can domesticate the mountain, but the sea is *feræ naturæ*. You may have a hut or know the owner of one, on the mountain-side; you see a light half-way up its ascent in the evening, and you know there is a home, and you might share it. You have noted certain trees, perhaps. You know the particular zone, where the hemlocks look so black in October when the maples and beeches have faded. All its reliefs and intaglios have electrotyped themselves in the medallions that hang round the walls of your memory's chamber. The sea remembers nothing. It is feline. It licks your feet; its huge flanks purr very pleasantly for you; but it will crack your bones, and eat you, for all that; and wipe the crimsoned foam from its jaws as though nothing had happened. The mountains give their lost children berries and water. The sea mocks their thirst and lets them die. The mountains have a grand, stupid, lovable tranquillity. The sea has a fascinating, treacherous intelligence. The mountains lie about us like huge ruminants, their broad backs awful to look upon, but safe to handle. The sea smooths its silver scales until you cannot see their joints; but their shining is that of a snake's belly, after all. In deeper suggestiveness, I find as great a difference. The mountains dwarf mankind, and foreshorten the procession of its long generations. The sea drowns out humanity and time; it has no sympathy with either, for it belongs to eternity; and of that it sings its monotonous song for ever and ever."

It was quite unnecessary for the writer of these words to state in set terms whether he loved best the mountains or the seaside. What we can domesticate, we love; what is foreign to our homes is very likely to be foreign to our hearts. To be sure, Longfellow preferred the seaside. He was born and passed his youth in one of the most delightful cities by the sea: in his own words:

"The beautiful town
That is seated by the sea."

The mountain air made him drowsy, so that on some Pittsfield days he could not get on at all with Kavanagh; which goes to confirm Dr. Holmes' liberal comment on the choice of a summer home; "the one where your place is, is the best for you.". . . "You must cut your climate to your constitution as much as much as your clothing to your shape. After this consult your taste and convenience. But if you would be happy in Berkshire you must carry mountains in your brain; and if you would enjoy Nahant you must have an ocean in your soul. Nature plays at dominos with you; you must match her piece or she will never give it up to you."

You will find more of this in the "Autocrat." Wonderful book that "Autocrat." More in it of the philosophy of the material, moral, intellectual, and spiritual universe, done up in a multitude of small packages, than are spread out over page upon page of a dozen ordinary books of great pretense. Whatever your case may be the Autocrat has a prescription for it.

Some of the paragraphs we have quoted explain in the Autocrat's own poetic, philosophic way the elements in the mountains, ever constant in form, ever varying in aspect, which give the regions they dominate a definite individuality, that fixes them in the memory of their children, to whom it doubly endears them.

While the present volume has been preparing, Pittsfield has received an unexpected, but perfectly natural and exceedingly welcome, testimonial to Dr. Holmes' remembered friendship. His son and namesake, Judge Holmes, found in the library left by him more than a thousand volumes; some of them duplicates of books already owned by himself, but mostly works— many of rare and curious value—better suited to the shelves of a public institution or of a writer upon such varied and often abstruse themes as Dr Holmes treated, than to those of one absorbed in intellectual pursuits of a different class; where they might long lie hidden and unused, while students were craving in vain the aid which they could give to their investigations. Judge Holmes did not wish this disuse, which would amount to a misuse, of the treasures which had fallen to him. Still less could he think of making merchandise of what had come to him from such a source. Remembering his father's old kindness for Pittsfield, and doubtless inheriting something of it, he therefore presented them to the Berkshire Athenæum, where they will long and conspicuously bear witness to the affection of the great author who once owned and enjoyed them for the town to which he was bound by many and varied ties.

This Athenæum is the "outward and visible manifestation" of what is best in intellectual Pittsfield. Its libraries, cabinets, and galleries are particularly rich in mementos of men distinguished in the higher fields of thought and action. Hitherto the most highly prized of these memorials, at least among those of men of letters, has been the desk upon which Hawthorne wrote his earlier and greatest novels. It is a plain but handsome piece of furniture; of solid mahogany; not large, but one can see, that, with its capacious lower drawers, a deal of hard literary work could be done upon it conveniently and comfortably. It looks as though it might very well have come from old Salem, and been the work-bench of a man like Hawthorne. The long and yearly increasing train of men and women who seek it as a shrine of genius is a pleasing testimony to the growth of the sentiment which prompts loving and admiring homage before it. It has long been the object first sought by visitors to the Athenæum of this class; although it might almost—not quite—have been said that it was only *primus inter pares*. But when the Holmes presentation shall have been arranged in the alcove to be prepared for it, the desk must be prepared to divide its honors with the books.

And this reminds us that, for the summer visitor to Berkshire the Athenæum is a capital supplement to its natural scenery. When a rainy day spoils his planned excursion in its fields and woods to some romantic spot, or his climbing for a grand view, it need not involve ennui in its cloudy hours; for they may be most agreeably spent in the enjoyment of the Athenæum's gathered treasures of art, nature, historic relics, and literature. Sometimes this affords a pleasing relief to the monotony of outdoor sight-seeing; and it always gives a keener relish for, and better understanding of, the landscapes afterward seen.

Our attention has just been called to another and very striking illustration of the enduring nature of Dr. Holmes' affection for his old own Berkshire home. It is contained in a letter to a very old and valued personal and literary friend, written as late as January 24, 1894. And it is worthy of remark that its three closely

THE NEW YORK
PUBLIC LIBRARY

PONTOOSUC LAKE.
(the yawk in the distance.)

filled pages were written by himself in his neat, firm penmanship, when most of his correspondence was carried on through his secretary. We can quote only a few sentences; but they are full of significance.

"Oh, how I should love to look on Pittsfield again! And yet I have always dreaded the rush of memories it would bring over me, and dread it still. But there lie buried many of my dearest and sweetest memories of my earlier middle age; and, if I cannot look on Greylock and Pontoosuc with these eyes which are fast growing dim, I can recall them with infinite affection and delight."

The poems collected in this little volume are far from the only ones that Dr. Holmes wrote in his seven Pittsfield summers. We have only taken those which have a decided Berkshire flavor. But there was an incident in the writing of one of the others—the "Astrea," if we remember rightly—which, though not unusual in the operation of busy minds, may be of instructive interest to some young writer. He had written one morning some thirty lines with more than his usual ease and rapidity. Then he "wrestled" long with a single couplet, of which he had a clear idea, but could not suit himself with the rhythm. The entrance of a casual visitor broke the "jam" of thought. The couplet was completed in a twinkling, and with a shout.

"Dr. Holmes made some pretty close studies, for use in his novels, of scenes and events which came under his eye in Pittsfield, and of the people who took part in them. Are you going to tell about those scenes and events and point out the originals of his characters?" No, inquiring friend. Very decidedly we are not going to do anything of the kind. Dr. Holmes certainly did witness some striking scenes here, ludicrous as well as otherwise; and he did depict them with a fidelity to nature that makes one suspect that he inherited the talents of some old Dutch artist far back in the Wendell genealogy. And he did make some portraits from life with like accurate truthfulness; so that an observant townsman, coming across one of these characters in his book, would be very apt to exclaim: "Why that is Mr. X, or old X, to a dot." And yet it might be that the novelist's character was given a birth-mark or a scar that did not disfigure the countenance of Mr. X. Novelists select and combine traits for their characters, just as the old Greek sculptor selected and combined the beauties of many beautiful women to form the most beautiful, and the representative of the goddess of beauty; only that it is not always beautiful traits that the novelist selects. Doubtless in the sculptor's work the beauty contributed by one model was so recognizable that in common report she received credit for all; and so with the originals from whom the novelist draws his characters; he whose most salient features most nearly correspond with the salient features of the man in the novel is held responsible for all the uglinesses with which the author may see fit to invest him; so that Mr. X may be wrongfully deformed with the humped back which properly belongs to Mr. Y.

There is yet another reason why it is particularly safe for us to refrain from attempting to identify the Pittsfield characters in Dr. Holmes' novels. While in his Berkshire verse there is as little harshness of thought as of rhythmical cadences, and while it is as void of censure as the sky is of clouds on the most perfect Berkshire day in June or September, there was in him abundant electricity; latent until it was needed for the purification of a moral atmosphere. Tolerant as his charitable philosophy was of the common frailties and errors of humanity, from the bottom of his heart he hated shams, hypocrisy, and the oppression of the helpless; and he lashed them without mercy wherever he found them hidden, even if it involved the "dusting" of a prominent citizen's best black broadcloth. If we should attempt to point out of what he made fun and whom he lashed, we might do injustice, and would certainly raise a storm that we do not care to face.

No; let who will solve the problem, Mr. X may still represent the unknown figure, for all we shall do to reveal him.

And now, to make a final quotation from the great and good-hearted doctor in medicine and in laws—" Good-by, old folks!"

HOUSE OF THE OLD CLOCK ON THE STAIRS.
Pittsfield, Mass., 1843.

APPENDIX.

THE OLD CLOCK ON THE STAIRS.

L'éternité est une pendule, dont le balancier dit et redit sans cesse ces deux mots seulement, dans le silence des tombeaux : "Toujours ! jamais ! Jamais ! toujours !"
JACQUES BRIDAINE.

Somewhat back from the village street
Stands the old-fashioned country seat.
Across its antique portico
Tall poplar trees their shadows throw,
And from its station in the hall
An ancient timepiece says to all,—
"Forever—never !
Never—forever !"

Half way up the stairs it stands,
And points and beckons with its hands
From its case of massive oak
Like a monk, who, under his cloak,
Crosses himself, and sighs, alas !
With sorrowful voice to all who pass,—
"Forever—never !
Never—forever !"

By day its voice is low and light;
But in the silent dead of night,
Distinct as a passing footstep's fall,
It echoes along the vacant hall,
Along the ceiling, along the floor,
And seems to say at each chamber door,—
      "Forever—never!
      Never—forever!"

Through days of sorrow and of mirth,
Through days of death and days of birth,
Through every swift vicissitude
Of changeful time, unchanged it has stood,
And as if, like God, it all things saw,
It calmly repeats those words of awe,—
      "Forever—never!
      Never—forever!"

In that mansion used to be
Free-hearted hospitality;
His great fires up the chimney roared;
The stranger feasted at his board;
But, like the skeleton at the feast,
That warning timepiece never ceased,—
      "Forever—never!
      Never—forever!"

There groups of merry children played,
There youths and maidens dreaming strayed;
O, precious hours! O, golden prime,
And affluence of love and time!
Even as a miser counts his gold,
Those hours the ancient timepiece told,—
      "Forever—never!
      Never—forever!"

From that chamber, clothed in white,
The bride came forth on her wedding night;
There, in that silent room below,
The dead lay in his shroud of snow;
And in the hush that followed the prayer,
Was heard the old clock on the stair,—
      "Forever—never!
      Never—forever!"

All are scattered now and fled, .
Some are married, some are dead;
And when I ask, with throbs of pain,
"Ah! when shall they all meet again?"
As in the days long since gone by,
The ancient timepiece makes reply,—
      "Forever—never!
      Never—forever!"

Never here, forever there,
Where all parting pain and care,
And death and time shall disappear,—
Forever there, but never here!
The horologe of Eternity
Sayeth this incessantly,—
      "Forever—never!
      Never—forever!"

There is a popular outcry just now against inserting in works intended for popular reading phrases in foreign languages without translations. The outcry is absurd, as of course every reader knows enough of French, German, and Latin to translate for himself; but as the demand seems to be in earnest we comply with it, so far as it concerns the quotation at the head of the poem of the old clock, which in English would read: "Eternity is a clock [horologe] whose pendulum says, and repeats without ceasing these two words only in the silence of the tombs: 'Forever! never! Never! forever!'" The context in the paragraph from which this quotation is taken makes it much more grim, but not so well adapted to the purpose of the poet.

The view of the House of the Old Clock, representing it as it was at the time of Mr. Longfellow's marriage, is copied from one presented to the Berkshire Athenæum a few years ago by his brother-in-law Nathan Appleton, and inscribed with the autograph signature of Henry W. Longfellow in testimony to its accuracy and his continued interest in the place.

A BERKSHIRE SUMMER MORNING.

ODE FOR THE BERKSHIRE JUBILEE.

By Mrs. Frances Ann Kemble.

Darkness upon the mountain and the vale.
The woods, the lakes, the fields, are buried deep,
In the still silent solemn star-watched sleep;
   No sound, no motion, and o'er hill and dale
   A calm and lovely death seems to embrace
Earth's fairest realms, and Heaven's unfathomed space.

   The forest slumbers, leaf and branch and bough,
High feathery crest, and lowliest grassy blade;
All restless, wandering wings, are folded now,
   That swept the sky, and in the sunshine play'd.
The lake's wild waves sleep in their rocky bowl.
Unbroken stillness streams from nature's soul,
And night's great, star-sown wings stretch o'er the whole.

In the deep trance of the hush'd universe,
The dark death mystery doth man rehearse;
Now, for a while, cease the swift thoughts to run
From task to task; tir'd labor, overdone
With lighter toil than that of brain or heart,
In the sweet pause of outward life takes part:
And hope, and fear, desire, love, joy, and sorrow,
Wait 'neath sleep's downy wings, the coming morrow.
Peace on the earth, profoundest peace in Heaven,
Praises the God of peace by whom 'tis given.

But hark! the woody depths of green
    Begin to stir;
Light breaths of life creep fresh between
    Oak, beech, and fir:
Faint rustling sounds of trembling leaves
    Whisper around;
The world at waking slowly heaves
    A sigh profound;
And showers of tears, night-gathered in her eyes,
Fall from fair nature's face, as she doth rise.

A ripple roughens on the lake,
The silver lilies shivering wake,
The leaden waves lift themselves up, and break,
    Along the laurel'd shore;
And woods and waters, answering each other, make
    Silence no more.

    And lo! the east turns pale!
    Night's dusky veil
      Thinner and thinner grows,
    Till the bright morning star,
      From hill to hill afar,
      His fire glance throws.
    Gold streaks run thro' the sky;
    Higher and yet more high
      The glory streams;
    Flushes of rosy hue
    Long lines of palest blue,
      And amber gleams,
      From the black valleys rise.
    The silver mists, like spray,
    Catch, and give back the ray,
      With thousand dyes.
Light floods the Heavens, light pours upon the earth;
In glorious light, the glorious day takes birth.

Hail to this day! that brings ye home,
  Ye distant wanderers from the mountain land.
Hail to this hour! that bids ye come
  Again upon your native hills to stand.
Hail, hail! From rocky peak,
  And wood embowered dale,
A thousand loving voices speak,
  Hail! home-turn'd pilgrims, hail!
Oh, welcome! From the meadow and the hill
    Glad greetings rise;
From flowing river, and from bounding rill,
Bright level lake, and dark green wood depths still,
And the sharp thunder-splinter'd crag, that strikes
    Its rocky spikes
    Into the skies.

Greylock, cloud-girdled, from his purple throne,
    A voice of welcome sends,
And from green sunny fields, a warbling tone
    The Housatonic blends.

Welcome ye absent long, and distant far!
  Who, from the roof-tree of your childhood turn'd,
Have waged mid strangers life's relentless war,
  While at your hearts, the ancient home-love burn'd.

Ye, that have plough'd the barren briny foam,
  Reaping hard fortunes from the stormy sea,
The golden grain fields rippling round your home,
  Roll their rich billows from all tempests free.

Ye, from those western, deadly blooming fields,
  Where Pestilence in Plenty's bosom lies,
The hardy rock-soil of your mountains yields
  Health's rosy blossoms to these purer skies.

And ye who on the accursed southern plain,
  Barren, not fruitful, with the sweat of slaves,
Have drawn awhile the tainted air in vain,
  'Mid human forms, their spirits' living graves.

Here, fall the fetters; by his cottage door
  Lord of the lordliest life, each peasant stands,
Lifting to God, as did his sires of yore,
  A heart of love and free laborious hands.*

On each bald granite brow, and forest crest,
  Each stony hill path, and each lake's smooth shore,
Blessings of noble exil'd patriots rest; †
  Liberty's altars are they evermore.

And on this air, there lingers yet the tone,
  Of those last sacred words to freedom given,
The mightiest utterance of that sainted one,
  Whose spirit from these mountains soar'd to Heaven.‡

Ye that have prosper'd, bearing hence with ye
  The virtues that command prosperity;
To the green threshold of your youth, ah! come!
  And hang your trophies round your early home.

Ye that have suffer'd, and whose weary eyes
  Have turn'd with sadness to your happier years,
Come to the fountain of sweet memories!
  And by its healing waters, dry your tears!

---

*This stanza was omitted in the reading, as it was thought not to be in strict harmony with the occasion.--ED.
† The exiled Italian patriots who were hospitably and sympathetically received by the Sedgwick family.
‡ Rev. Dr. William Ellery Channing.

Ye that departed young, and old return,
 Ye who led forth by hope—now hopeless come,
If still, unquenched within your hearts, doth burn
 The sacred love and longing for your home:

> Hail, hail! Bright hill and dale
> With joy resound!
> Join in the joyful strain!
> Ye have not wept in vain.
> The parted meet again,
> The lost shall yet be found!

And may God guard thee, oh, thou lovely land!
 Danger, nor evil, nigh thy borders come.
Green towers of freedom may thy hills still stand.
 Still, be each valley, peace and virtue's home:
The stranger's grateful blessing rest on thee,
 And firm as Heaven, be thy prosperity!

A QUAINT OLD PAPER.

AFTER all the preceding pages were in type, we received, through the courtesy of Mr. Henry Talcott Mills, from Miss Electa Colt, an old manuscript found among the papers of her father, the late Hon. Ezekiel Root Colt, who was much given to preserving such "curios" of Berkshire's old times. And it is of so peculiar interest that we add it here, even at this late hour. We have endeavored, in our chapter illustrating Dr. Holmes' poem of "The Ploughman," to give the reader some idea of the quaint elements of strength which rendered the old Berkshire Agriculture Society a source of rational pleasure to many thousands of men, women and children; and of power for good in the world. But this old paper makes one of its early cattle-show anniversaries a delicious reality for us; the dead past is in verity restored to life. It contains, in his own penmanship, the directions for this anniversary given to his lieutenants by Elkanah Watson, the creator of the great system of American county cattle-shows. In it, we can, as it were, see his mind in full operation as he was laying the foundations of that system; even as, when the first cattle-show procession was passing through Pittsfield streets, the spectators saw Abraham Scholfield's hand-looms at work.

Half of the old paper preserved by Mr. Colt is occupied by a ground-plan of the old meeting-house of 1791, in which the exercises were held. There is a broad platform before the pulpit—the deacons' seat intervening—upon which places are assigned for the officers of the society; those for the president, vice-president and a third person—perhaps a chaplain—being designated by a drawing which is supposed to represent a sofa, but which looks much more like a boat with three oarsmen. The body of the auditorium is arranged in five sections: the pews on the west side of the broad middle aisle being divided between the "male" and the "female" premium-takers, and those on the east side being reserved for the members of the society, while the outer rows are left for the "spectators." We copy the directions verbatim.

"CEREMONY.—The President to call off the premiums,—The Vice-President to hand the article to the President,—the treasurer to take it from him—the person [to whom the premium is awarded] to advance to the foot of the stage, as his name is called: if a lady, to be met by a marshal and conducted,—the treasurer to descend the steps, meet her at the foot, and deliver to her the premium and certificate |of merit]—the marshal then to conduct her to a pew on the right.—If a gentleman, he is to ascend the steps, and receive his premium from the President; the marshal then to conduct him to a west pew, designated above.—An elegant band of music to be provided in the gallery,— some lasses as singers to be trained to sing some pastoral airs, draped in appropriate garlands and flowers, as each premium is delivered to the ladies. Yankee Doodle is to be struck up |as each male premium-taker is called| to continue until he reaches the foot of the stage; and then cease. A full band to play some favorite short air after the premiums are delivered to the men—also the women."

We see traces of Mr. Watson's Parisian training transferred to all this rural pomp and circumstance; and to those who do not take into consideration its object it may seem out of place on such an occasion. It would be so at the present day, to which a balloon ascension or a gubernatorial lion is better adapted; but it was not so in the old days, when rude pageantry was loved if it was significant. Sentiment is at all times a powerful motor for the public mind. And there was certainly more sentiment in a silver bowl or a dozen teaspoons, even if only the workmanship of the village silversmith, if delivered according to the old programme quoted above, and with a handsomely printed certificate of merit, than there is in the one, ten, or more dollars delivered as they now are to meritorious premium-takers at our cattle-shows. At any rate the old-time cattle-show pageantries made the desired impression upon the secluded community of few holidays, whose only other similar spectacle in the year was the procession of the judges in their robes, from the tavern where they "stopped," to the court-house, preceded by the high sheriff in uniform and holding a naked sword before him. The impression made by those old cattle-shows extended far and wide, as thousands of others were modeled upon them; and their influence for good is felt to-day. In this year 1895, Berkshire county is witnessing festal occasions— some of them at the very moment we are writing these words—of far greater costliness and splendor than even Elkanah Watson's sanguine forecast of the county's future could have conceived. Will they, three-quarters of a century hence, be remembered, and be worthy of memory for their influence upon the world, as the programme we have quoted recalls the old cattle-show exercises of so long ago that they were already a fading phantom of the past when Dr. Holmes read his "Ploughman" in the same old

meeting-house in which they were conducted?
It may be; for

> "Moves one, move all;
> Hark to the footfall!
> On, on forever."

PITTSFIELD, June 6, 1895.

www.ingramcontent.com/pod-product-compliance
Lightning Source LLC
Chambersburg PA
CBHW030820190426
43197CB00036B/640